Entering a Child's World

Narrative Pedagogy in Early Childhood Art Education

Pamela Grace Krakowski

Wisdom of Practice Series
Learning Moments Press
Oakmont, PA

Entering a Child's World:
Narrative Pedagogy in Early Childhood Art Education

Published by Learning Moment Press
Publishing Arm of Scholar-Practitioner Nexus
Oakmont, PA 15139

scholarpractitionernexus.com

ISBN 979-8-9860800-1-7

The tree drawing on the front cover was created by Anna, age 5. Fascinated by the tree's apples, she drew them on the tree and ground, capturing the feeling of "appleness."

BISAC Subject:
EDU 057000 Arts in Education
EDU 050000 Collaborative & Team Teaching
Onix Audience Code: 06 Professional & Scholarly

Book Layout: Mike Murray, Pearhouse Productions, pearhouse.com

*To children everywhere who like
to make things with their hands.*

"When everything goes right, a mobile is a piece of poetry that dances with the joy of life..."

JEAN PAUL SARTRE DESCRIBING
A MOBILE OF ALEXANDER CALDER

Table of Contents

List of Figures

Prologue

I became interested in narrative pedagogy—although I did not call it that at the time—when I began my first full-time teaching job at a residential school for children with blindness. I remember my first day of school, waiting anxiously for my first class to arrive. Coming down the hallway to the art room were four adolescent boys, blind from birth. They greeted me and found their seats at a table where I had prepared slabs of clay, along with natural materials and tools for making textures. Since I had never taught art to children with blindness, my intention was to observe how they approached the clay as a material. To my surprise, the boys were not interested in exploring all the possible textures the tools could make. Instead, they began to associate memories and stories with the textures they created. Tim scratched a piece of clay with a toothbrush and made a rough surface. "This reminds me of my uncle's beard. I hate it when my uncle hugs me with that scratchy old beard."

"I know what you mean," said Devin, sitting next to him. "You'd think he'd at least shave." Devin then picked up a wooden dowel rod and began poking holes into his slab of clay. "This hole reminds me of when I fell into the ditch on my mobility lesson the other day. That was so scary."

As I watched and listened to the boys sharing their experiences, I observed that they were not exploring "texture for texture's sake" or texture as an element of design. Instead, they used the physical properties of clay and other materials as a language through which to tell the stories of experience and memory. As a novice teacher, I realized immediately that they were the experts in their world without sight, and

I was the stranger. If I were to connect art meaningfully to their lives, I would need to listen very closely and try my best to see things from their point of view. Through empathy, I would need to enter their world.

A few years later, on another first day of school, I was waiting for my first preschool class to arrive. Instead of teenage boys coming down the hallway to my art classroom were three childcare assistants, four-year old Talia, and three other preschoolers, all blind from birth. Talia's classroom teacher had warned me that Talia was not going to like art. "She kicks and screams anytime she thinks someone is going to ask her to touch an art material."

I had prepared the environment for an unstructured exploration of art materials so that I could observe how the children approached them. I had set out lotions, warm water, and other soothing "pre-art" materials that would be less threatening to touch. After an opening song and movement game, I invited the children to explore the materials. Talia started to scream.

In the weeks that followed, I decided to play with Talia without using any art materials. I hoped that by building a trusting relationship, she would grow more courageous in her explorations with materials. Then one day it happened, when Talia was playing with a baby doll. "Would you like to give the baby a bath?" I asked, hoping she would want to play in the water.

"Nope," she responded without hesitation.

"Would your baby like some lotion on her tummy?"

Silence.

"I think I'll rub some lotion on my baby's tummy," I said.

Silence. Talia was listening.

I rubbed lotion on the doll I held and sang a lullaby-like song. Talia reached out to feel what I was doing and touched the lotion. This time she did not scream or pull back.

"Would your baby like some lotion on her tummy?" I asked again.

She was still silent. And then she held out one finger. I gently rubbed some lotion on her one finger, and she rubbed it on her doll and began to sing a lullaby to her doll.

In the weeks and months that followed, Talia allowed me to enter her world of make-believe and art making. Her one finger exploration led to smothering her baby doll with lotion. "This baby is learning to like lotion. She didn't like it at first." she told me. Eventually Talia began to explore finger—and then feet painting—with lotion. Gradually we moved on to investigating new materials—warm water in a tub to give her baby a bath—and eventually to "riskier" materials—paint, glue, and clay. At the end of the school year, I would have never guessed that Talia had ever screamed and kicked at the very mention of an art material.

Although I did not use the words narrative pedagogy at the time, when I look back at both first-day of school experiences, I saw that Tim, Devin, and Talia[1] showed me the importance of listening to their narratives and understanding children's experiences from their point of view. The children had become my guides, introducing me to their unsighted world. To engage them further in meaningful art making, I had to understand how they navigated their world, how they constructed concepts without vision, and how they approached making art through their other senses. They showed me that story, play, experience, and art materials were tightly woven together, and that meaningful art making was, for them, not learning about the elements and principles of design. When I ignored their experiences and followed unquestioningly my own "sighted person's" agenda, I found that I did not connect as well, and important opportunities for meaningful learning were lost. The lessons the children taught me shaped my pedagogy for years to come, in ways I only later began to understand.

---

1 Throughout the book, all names of the children have been changed to protect their privacy,

CHAPTER 1

Teaching Art in a Narrative Frame of Mind

Pedagogical tact is "the expression of a thoughtfulness that involves the total being of the person, an active sensitivity toward the subjectivity of the others, for what is unique and special about the other person."

MAX VAN MANEN

In the *Tact of Teaching*, Max van Manen contends that educators who cultivate certain sensibilities embody a practical and mindful orientation toward children and their well-being. Such sensibilities cannot be learned as behavioral principles, methods, or techniques. Rather they constitute embodied knowledge that can be cultivated through greater awareness of one's way of being with and responding to students.

This book represents my quest to understand more explicitly and more deeply the pedagogical and aesthetic sensibilities I bring to my practice of early childhood art education. I have framed this quest as an exploration of the tensions between normative and narrative pedagogy. *Normative pedagogy* refers to what I believe **ought** to be happening in the classroom—what I want to see happening. It is my notion of the curriculum—my aims, goals, objectives, specific lesson plans, expectations, and values. It is what I believe is "true, beautiful, good, and just,"[1] and what I believe is worth teaching. *Narrative pedagogy* refers to what *is* happening in the classroom. It entails listening closely to children and allowing their ideas, interests, stories, and experiences to shape the direction of the curriculum. When I follow their narrative inclinations, the art experience seems to be deeply satisfying and meaningful for both the children and me.

A Metaphor for Balancing the Normative and the Narrative

When I first began thinking about normative and narrative pedagogies, I bordered on presenting a false dichotomy between the two. Over time, however, I began to see a dynamic tension between them, because I value *both* the narrative and the normative. What my students have to say is important, and I have a body of knowledge, skills, and concepts that I believe are important for them to learn. As I reflected on this duality, the image of a mobile came to me; more specifically, the mobiles created by American artist Alexander Calder. Art educator Elliot Eisner comments, "a metaphor makes public that which is ineffable."[2] The concept of Calder's mobiles served this purpose for me.

A mobile comprises many elements held in a state of balance by tensions exerted on horizontal and vertical wires. Creating this balance depends upon the artist's capacity to sense the weight of various elements and to adjust the placement of wires by drawing upon experience, intuition, an embodied understanding of materials, a feeling for coherence, an eye for color, and a playfulness with form. In Calder's mobiles, I found a metaphor for recognizing and cultivating the sensibilities necessary for balancing the normative and the narrative elements of my teaching—in any situation, at any moment. If I give too much weight to my normative agenda, the children's narrative is thrown out of kilter. Conversely, giving excessive weight to the children's narrative may displace the normative.

---

1   Wanda T. May, *"Teachers as Curriculum Developers,"* in *Context, Content, and Community in Art Education: Beyond Postmodernism,* ed. R.W. Neperud (Albany, NY: State University of New York Press, 1995), 59.
2   Elliot W. Eisner, *The Educational Imagination* (New York: Macmillan, 1979), 200.

The very essence of a mobile is motion; it is always in a state of flux, subject to the force of air currents. Every time one element moves, it sets the other elements in motion. So too, are the elements in the art classroom in motion. Air currents stirring the normative and narrative elements of the art classroom encompass both constant and unexpected pressures. Constant pressures, for example, include large classes, limited budgets, inadequate space, insufficient time, academic standards, and similar school demands. Unexpected pressures might be a unilateral administrative mandate to teach a particular curriculum, the first day of school, 9/11, family sickness or trauma, the sudden emergence of a deadly virus, or the premiere of *Star Wars*. Unexpected pressures can arise from the changing needs, interests, moods, thoughts, feelings, and concerns of students and teacher. All such pressures are at play within the larger currents of popular culture. Balancing the normative and the narrative elements in the face of such pressures is not easy. It requires a constellation of sensibilities that, taken together, constitute a narrative frame of mind. Maintaining a narrative frame of mind allows me to enter the children's worlds of imagination, play, and artmaking and to introduce into those worlds the lessons I hope to teach.

Purpose of the Book

Embodied sensibilities are not as easily recognized and described as technical knowledge and methods. Yet, they often play a far greater role in the life of the art classroom than we might realize. For this reason, my purpose in writing this book is to make these embodied sensibilities more explicit and visible. In doing so, I aim to explicate what I mean by a narrative frame of mind and illustrate the fundamental role it plays in maintaining a balance between normative and narrative pedagogies.

Although both normative and narrative pedagogies involve technical knowledge and skills, I resonate with van Manen's view that pedagogy is more than a "dutiful execution of technical acts," or merely a "body of knowledge" that the teacher possesses. Rather, pedagogy is a *knowing body*—an empathic, responsive way of being with students that recognizes what actions are appropriate in each moment with a particular child or class.[3] Educators Michael Connelly and Jean Clandinin call this personal practical knowledge.[4] Social scientists Barry Schwartz and Kenneth Sharpe characterize this capacity for responsiveness as practical wisdom.[5] I think of this as a narrative frame of mind guided by pedagogical and aesthetic sensibilities.

For me, cultivating a narrative frame of mind entails looking inward. In *The Courage to Teach*, Parker Palmer makes this point quite eloquently:

> Teaching, like any human activity, emerges from one's inwardness, for better or worse. As I teach, I project my condition of my soul onto my students, my subject, and our way of being together. The entanglements I experience in the classroom are often no more or less than the convolutions of my inner life. Viewed from this angle, teaching holds a mirror to the soul. If I am willing to look in that mirror and not run from what I see, I have a chance to gain self-knowledge—and knowing myself is as crucial to good teaching as knowing my students and my subject.
>
> In fact, knowing my students and my subject depends heavily on self-knowledge. When I do not know myself, I cannot know who my students are. I will see them through a glass darkly, in the shadows of my unexamined life—and when I cannot see them clearly, I cannot teach them well. When I do not know myself, I cannot know my subject—not at the deepest levels of embodied, personal meaning.[6]

---

3   Robert K. Brown, "Max van Manen and Pedagogical Human Science Research," in *Understanding Curriculum as Phenomenological and Deconstructed Text, eds.* William. F. Pinar and William M. Reynolds (New York: Teachers College Press, 1992), 56.

4   F. Michael Connelly, and D. Jean Clandinin, *Teachers as Curriculum Planners: Narratives of Experience* (New York: Teachers College Press, 1988).

5   Barry Schwartz and Kenneth Sharpe, *Practical Wisdom: The Right Way to Do the Right Thing* (New York: Riverhead Books, 2010).

6   Parker J. Palmer, *The Courage to Teach* (San Francisco, CA: Jossey-Bass, 1998), 2.

In the remainder of this book, I hold a mirror up to my pedagogical practice. At times, the images reflected are quite affirming; they help me understand more clearly the intuitive moves I make when in a narrative frame of mind. Other images are surprising, even shocking, as they reveal air currents—forces—that overwhelm my capacity to enter the children's worlds. By exploring these images, my aim is not to be self-deprecating or self-congratulatory. Rather, it is to enter a process that Linda Darling Hammond and Jeannie Oakes call "deep learning."[7] While the lessons I learn are about my own embodied knowledge, they are also about pedagogical and aesthetic sensibilities that can empower any art teacher to cultivate a narrative frame of mind.

Organization of the Book

In the remainder of the book, I share vignettes of my early childhood teaching practice in a K-8, private, laboratory school on the urban campus of a major university. The vignettes are drawn from a study I completed with students in my kindergarten, first, and second grade classes, which the National Association for the Education of Young Children (NAEYC) considers to be the older end of the ages of early childhood education. It is worth noting, that as Joseph Tobin suggests:

> Many non-progressive schools emphasize academics in the kindergarten and primary grades—a "trickle down" approach—however, early childhood educators need to resist this academic pressure and push for a "trickle up" into the elementary curriculum of rich multisensory experiences, less worksheets, and more free play.[8]

Each chapter begins with a description of the *Pedagogical Considerations* that provide the context for classroom events. The events are presented as *Vignettes* portraying what unfolds as I set my lesson plans in motion. The Vignettes are followed by *Balancing*

7   Linda Darling Hammond, and Jeannie Oakes, *Preparing Teachers for Deeper Learning* (San Francisco: John Wiley & Sons, 2005).
8   Joseph Tobin, Ed. Making a Place for Pleasure in Early Childhood Education (New Haven: Yale University Press, 1997), 6.

Sensibilities, a section in which I explore "air currents" that are stirring narrative and normative elements during the lesson. In some vignettes, the air currents create enough pressure to undermine my narrative frame of mind. In other vignettes, my intuitions allow me to maintain a balance between the normative and the narrative.

Chapters 2 and 3 contrast two different experiences that occurred in the context of a local art museum. The first explores pressures that overwhelmed my narrative frame of mind; the second illustrates embodied knowledge that allowed me to enter the children's world. The latter represents what I view as the most magical moment in my teaching experience.

Chapters 4 and 5 explore my struggles to balance my own views of appropriate artmaking and the importance of my students' imaginations. In these vignettes, my aesthetic sensibilities came into tension with the aesthetic sensibilities of the children.

Chapters 6 and 7 focus on ways my narrative frame of mind prompted me to create safe and welcoming spaces for young children, while Chapters 8 and 9 illustrate the art classroom as a play space in which children can engage in their natural inclinations for play, storytelling, and art making. Chapter 10 presents one final vignette in which I revisit a year-long collaboration in which a classroom teacher and I carried out an integrated science and art curriculum.

In Chapter 11—*Cultivating Aesthetic Sensibilities*, I look at the Aesthetic Sensibilities associated with a narrative frame of mind. These sensibilities are clustered under the concepts of Aesthetic Vision, The Rightness of Fit, Improvising the Dance of Shapes, Holding the Tension of Opposites, Imagining and Playing with Possibilities, and Experiencing Aesthetic Satisfaction. I conclude with the lessons that I learned about cultivating and deepening these sensibilities.

CHAPTER 2

Art Class in the Museum

TEACHING AT THE INTERSECTION OF PRIVATE AND PUBLIC SPACES

*What visitors bring with them adds to their experience
in the museum...*

CATHERINE STAINTON

PEDAGOGICAL CONSIDERATIONS

Introducing children to traditional and contemporary art masterpieces is part of my normative pedagogy. Fortunately, I can include field trips to a world class art museum located a short distance from the laboratory school. Planning a lesson for a museum trip, however, is fraught with several pressures and expectations. Children, who naturally learn through their bodies and senses, are not allowed to touch the art, to run, or to use loud voices. The museum staff needs to know where I will be at all times. Therefore, I have to adhere closely to a detailed timeline. Additionally, there are pressures of teaching in a public setting where onlookers can observe the children and me.

All these pressures can potentially disturb the balance between the normative and narrative. The following vignette depicts how fear swept away narrative sensibilities.

When I take children to an art museum, I want them to have a meaningful, engaging encounter with a work of art. I want the learning experience to be pleasurable so that they will have a strong emotional desire to return with family and friends. I believe that it is possible for them to experience what museum educators call a *flow* experience and what artists describe as having a *relationship* with a work of art— to have a painting as a friend. Meaningful, engaging experiences for young children are more likely to happen when they respond to only one or two works of art at a time, through ways of coming to know that are natural for them—play, creative dramatics, movement, storytelling, art making, and age-appropriate discussions. Whenever I plan a lesson for a museum visit, I hope to open possibilities for this to happen.

Through years of experience, I can tightly script a lesson plan that adheres to the strict guidelines of teaching in a museum. At the same time, I know how to be improvisational. I had acquired many "methods" for helping young children look at and talk about art. I relish the feeling of being able to hold their attention in the palms of my hands.

Thus, fully confident, I began planning a perfect field trip. The K-1-2 children were in the middle of a deep exploration of gardening and plants. What an ideal time to introduce them to Claude Monet who loved to garden! How fortunate that our museum owns one of Monet's water lily paintings, a work so large that our whole class could sit in front of it and make art. How perfect that I own "Linnea in Monet's Garden," a wonderful children's video about a little girl who visits Monet's house, gardens, and water lily paintings. How perfect that I own a puppet that looks like Monet and a picture book that introduces children to the idea of walking into an Impressionist painting and having it come to life.

I decided to do a variation on an art project that had previously worked well with children of this age. We would make miniature, three-dimensional Monet museums with little stand up finger puppets of family and friends as museum visitors. The museums would serve as a memory of our experience. They also would provide a way for the children to connect more meaningfully to Monet's water lily painting. The added element of playing with the puppets would engage the children even more deeply. Several family members would accompany us on this museum adventure.

VIGNETTE—IN FRONT OF THE MONET

Pedagogical Enactment—Part 1

On Monday morning, I met with the children in their homeroom to introduce the lesson. They enjoyed watching "Linnea in Monet's Garden"; they loved the idea of making miniature museums, and they couldn't wait to go on the field trip. I told them that today we would make our family and friends finger puppets for our museums.

I passed out the paper for the puppets, and the children eagerly began to draw. A group of five boys raised their hands. "Can we draw Darth Vader?" The boys had been drawing *Star Wars* characters for weeks and could think of nothing else. Without pausing, I immediately responded, "No. Family and friends only."

The boys looked disappointed but went back to drawing, somewhat halfheartedly. Ignoring their looks, I rationalized that I gave them plenty of opportunities to draw *Star Wars* characters. If I allowed Darth Vader to meet Claude Monet, all sorts of violence might erupt in the boys' artwork. I wanted to create a peaceful atmosphere when we visited Monet's painting of water lilies—not an attack from outer space. I did not give my decision a second thought.

Pedagogical Enactment—Part 2

The day of the field trip arrived. In the Impressionist gallery, all 24 children and 12 adults settled themselves on the floor in front of a very long painting of Monet's water lilies. Looking out over the sea of faces, I wondered if I would be able to keep their attention. All eyes were on me. I pulled out my Claude Monet puppet with the hope of engaging them. My *"Star Wars"* boys were squirmy and chatty. The puppet began by talking to them in French.

"Bonjour! Je m'apelle Monsieur Claude Monet."

The children became quiet. I whispered in Monet's
ear. "Pssst! Monsieur Monet, you are speaking French.
The children don't understand what you're saying."

"Oh, you're right," he said, acting a bit confused.
"Where am I?"

"Pittsburgh!" the children yelled out.

"Pittsburgh?" Claude Monet responded, "You must
speak English then. I'm sorry. I'm very old, and I'm
a little hard of hearing. And you—you're a little hard
to see." The puppet, Monsieur Monet, looked out over
his audience. "You look a little like blotches of color
to me."

The children laughed, remembering from the "Linnea" video how
a close view of Monet's water lily paintings looked like blotches of
color.

The lesson progressed. Monsieur Monet read the book, *Katy
and the Impressionists,* and the children, pretended to walk into the
painting (like in the book) and describe what they saw and what they
imagined hiding underneath the lily pads. They became animated in
their discussion. However, since many of them had difficulty listening
to each other share their ideas, I felt as if I was beginning to lose their
attention—and control. After a few more minutes of discussion, I
moved on, hoping I would refocus them and crossing my fingers that I
would not forget my pedagogical script.

Monsieur Monet and I introduced the next step—making miniature
Impressionist-like paintings of imaginary gardens for our museums.
Our discussion of all the colors that we saw when we pretended to
walk into his water lily garden painting became our inspiration for
experimenting with blending colors. I had chosen oil pastels for our
medium because of the Impressionist-like qualities their marks made. I
engaged the children in a demonstration of different ways to blend the
oil pastels and then invited them to create their own paintings.

Immediately, nineteen of the children and their parents began
experimenting with enthusiasm. I noticed, however, that my five

Star War boys were not interested in the water lily painting or the art project. The other children worked intently for the next 45 minutes. The five boys made a few marks and announced that they were done. In typical art teacher fashion, I sat down next to them and tried to get them to experiment more with the oil pastels. Again, they added a few more marks and then made sure I knew that they were "really" done. When I realized I could no longer get them to work on their museums, I reluctantly said they could draw whatever they wanted. Not surprisingly, all of them started drawing their favorite scenes from *Star Wars*.

As I watched them, I sensed my heart sinking. I had the unsettling realization I had made a big mistake by not letting them create *Star War* characters for their puppets on Monday. Deep within, the gnawing "what if" questions began to haunt me. What if I had let them draw Darth Vader, would they have connected to the painting in a more meaningful way? Would I have been able to engage them? Why had I been so inflexible? Everything had been so well thought out. What went wrong?

BALANCING SENSIBILITIES

Reflecting on this lesson, I saw that my *fears*—fear of failure in front of others, fear of not looking good, fear of not being a good enough art teacher—kept me from responding in a narrative frame of mind. I had failed to create what Parker Palmer called an *open* learning space, where the children could interact personally with the Monet painting through their artmaking, which was, after all, my broader normative aim. Why was I fearful and how did my fears influence what happened?

The first inklings of anxiety had begun when Alicia, the children's classroom teacher, told me that nine parents would be accompanying us. That's wonderful, I thought. For years I had wanted to plan a museum field trip like this with parents and their children. My hope was that families would feel so comfortable in the galleries that they would want to make return visits. As I read through the list, however, I recognized the name of a well-known art therapist in the city. What if I "mess up" in front of her? What if I mess up in front of all the parents? This was the most difficult early childhood class I had ever taught. Twelve out of 24 of the children seemed to have difficulty interacting socially. Two had difficulty speaking English. Many needed very clear boundaries. Only a few could sit still for a few minutes. Many were impulsive and talked out frequently. It was a class that left me exhausted.

Fear set in. I began to envision the children running around out of control, knocking over sculptures, touching the paintings, and throwing oil pastels. How could I keep their attention? What had I been thinking?

NARRATIVE SENSIBILITY

Acknowledging the vulnerability inherent in the public space of teaching can help us to better manage the performance anxiety that can undermine a narrative frame of mind.

Why, I asked myself, was I taking such an unpredictable group to the museum? I must be crazy.

To allay my fears, I made a preliminary visit to the museum and carefully scripted my lesson. I also planned everything that I needed to say—just in case stage fright set in. I carefully thought through each activity to keep the children engaged. I left the museum with my confidence restored. Unfortunately, I failed to consider one important fact.

The weekend before the field trip, the new *Star Wars* movie—*The Phantom Menace*—arrived on the scene. For the past year my students had waited expectantly for it, drawing *Star Wars* images every chance they got. I loved *Star Wars*, too, and had seen the movie on opening night. I kept many of the action figures in the art classroom for the children to play with and sketch. However, with all of my attention on planning the perfect field trip, it never occurred to me that Luke Skywalker and Darth Vader would be dominating my students' minds.

I had done everything possible to make a fail-safe lesson. Although I would have planned the lesson in detail regardless of the parents, I was driven to plan so that I would feel safe—to make sure that I did not fall flat on my face in front of the other adults. In my journal, I wrote:

> *I did not know it at the time, but I slipped into performance mode, where I wanted to win the*

approval of my parent-audience. I wanted to be seen as a good art teacher. As a result, I was too afraid, even paralyzed, by the thought of stepping out on a limb and changing my lesson plan in midstream. I was frozen. What if something unexpected happened and I couldn't control the class? I was gripped by the fear of looking bad, of not being able to control the children. Because I had been an experienced museum educator for 20 years, I put even more pressure on myself to make sure the lesson did not fall apart. What would it say about me as an experienced teacher if I couldn't handle this class in the museum?

In his book, T*he Courage to Teach*, Parker Palmer observes that "teaching [is] a daily exercise in vulnerability," because it always takes place "at the dangerous intersection of personal and public life."[1] It is at this dangerous intersection where we make ourselves vulnerable to being judged or ridiculed. More than anything, he states, teachers fear appearing ignorant to themselves and to others. Palmer emphasizes from his own experience that the more he fears his "backstage ineptitude [will] be exposed," the more he tries to make his "onstage performance slicker and smoother."[2] When this happens, he believes his students are less likely to learn what he desires for them. In the following passage about writer Jane Tompkins, Palmer addresses the importance in his own life of bridging the divide between his on-stage and backstage life:

> One of my favorite essays on teaching is Jane Tompkins', *Pedagogy of the Distressed*.[3] It seems to have written directly to my divided condition. With wonderful candor, Tompkins says that her obsession as a teacher had not been with helping students learn what they wanted and needed to know but rather with "(a) showing the students how smart I was; (b) showing them how knowledgeable I was; and (c) showing them how well prepared I was for class. I had been putting

---

1   Palmer, 17.
2   Palmer, 29.
3   Jane Tompkins, "Pedagogy of the Distressed," *College English* 52, no. 6 (1991).

on a performance whose true goal was not to help the students learn but to act in such a way that the students would have a good opinion of me."

Then she asks, "How did our main goal turn out to be performance?" Her answer rings true to me—fear: "Fear of being shown up for what you are: a fraud, stupid, ignorant, a clod, a dolt, a sap, a weakling, someone who can't cut the mustard."[4]

Palmer's and Thompkins' comments ring true for me. My inability to waiver from my preplanned lesson allowed me to hide behind teaching methods and techniques. I resonate with Palmer's view that in a profession such as ours, we often fear exposure and seek safety behind the technical.

As I wrote in my journal, my fear of failure increased my need to control:

When I am being observed and evaluated by my supervisor or another adult in the classroom whom I want to impress or please, the focus came off the children and onto how well was I doing. What were the other adults in the room thinking? Would I make a mistake? Would I look good? Would the children look good? Would the children make me look good? The children's performance then became a reflection of whether I was a good teacher or not. Hence, I needed to control their behavior.

A similar situation had occurred when a particular art lesson did not go as planned as I taught in front of a new student teacher. As I sensed the children's frustration with the activity, I began to freeze up. Instead of changing my plan and adjusting to the children, I dug my heels in deeper, trying to control the lesson and its outcome. The children resisted even more. Elementary art educator Wendy Milne, in a study of

---

4   Palmer, 28-29.

her pedagogy, wrote about a similar phenomenon. She noted that when she tried to be *in control* of what the children made, she ended up *out of control*, because her art students resisted being told what to do.[5]

My fear of failure and need to control forced me to impose my ideas on the boys, ignoring how they wanted their Monet museums to be. As Palmer wrote, when teachers feel insecure, they are driven to pack the learning space with their words and ideas, not the children's. By having the

> **NARRATIVE SENSIBILITY**
>
> Understanding that the excessive need for security and control can result in losing control over what really matters.

children create only family and friends for their puppets, I limited their artistic visions from emerging. If I had listened to what the boys were trying to tell me—that they loved *Star Wars*—that it was the most important thing in their lives to draw at that moment—that it was a theme that emotionally consumed them—I might have seen possible connections. Unfortunately, my fear of failure and need for control inhibited my ability to think creatively. Would it have been so terrible for Darth Vader to be part of their museum? Or for Darth Vader to visit Monet's water lily painting? So, what if the boys used *Star Wars* imagery instead of garden imagery? Darth Vader could have stolen the Monet painting, and we needed to create our own Impressionist-like painting in its place for our museums. Or if I had been really daring, I could have let the boys draw their own Impressionistic-like Star Wars landscapes.

Csikszentmihalyi[6] contends that creativity flourishes in a nonjudgmental atmosphere where one feels free to take risks and make mistakes. Leaving the privacy and safety of my classroom and entering the public space of the museum, I lost the flexibility to respond "in the moment." Ironically, ignoring the children's narrative undermined my normative agenda of making the museum experience intrinsically motivating by tapping into the learner's interests and life experiences. As Max van Manen reminds me, "…deep meaningful learning cannot

---

5   Wendy M. Milne, *Professional Learning through Reflective Artmaking: A Pedagogical Portfolio* (Oakmont: Learning Moments Press, 2021).
6   Mihaly Csikszentmihalyi, *Flow: The Psychology of Optimal Experience* (New York: Harper Collins, 1990).

take place in the absence of interest." Interest is not a state of mind that children conjure up upon request. Rather, "to be interested [is] to be intensely present to something or somebody. A subject that interests [the child] was a subject that matters to [the child]."[7] Similarly, Dewey discussed the importance of nurturing a habit of mind that he called *wholeheartedness*. Too often, children's interests are compartmentalized:

> A pupil gives an external, perfunctory attention to the teacher and to his book and lesson while his inmost thoughts are concerned with matters more attractive to him. He pays attention with ear or eye, but his brain is occupied with affairs that make an immediate appeal.[8]

The boys displayed wholeheartedness when they drew their *Star Wars* characters. It was my responsibility as a teacher to listen to their interests and discover how to connect what mattered most to them to the subject of art.

Without minimizing my failure to respond in a narrative frame of mind, I did eventually come to the realization that the lesson—if not perfect—was at least good enough. In the final analysis, 19 of the 24 children had responded with enthusiasm. My planning had been based on past experiences where I *had* listened to the children's narrative and learned about their interests, responses, and understandings. When I was in tune to my emotions and memories of what the children responded to in the past, I could draw from those memories when lesson planning.

Even though my fears choked my intuition during the Monet lesson, it did surface later, telling me, "Something's not right." The sensibility of intuition was valuable in achieving balance between the narrative and the normative whether it surfaced in the moment or after the fact. When the narrative and normative become imbalanced, I am not always able to restore balance during a particular lesson. However, if I follow my hunch that something does not feel right, I can try to create a balance in subsequent lessons. In most instances, there are second chances.

---

7   Max van Manen, *The Tact of Teaching: The Meaning of Pedagogical Thoughtfulness* (Albany, NY: State University of New York Press, 1991), 196.
8   John Dewey, *How We Think* (New York: D. C. Heath & Co., 1933), 31.

Two days after the museum trip, during their regularly scheduled art class, I offered the boys the option of making more puppets of whomever they wanted. Cheers went up from four of the five boys. They ran to the front of the room and grabbed new pieces of paper on which to draw Darth Vader and his enemies. My hunch that they needed to have more freedom of choice with

NARRATIVE SENSIBILITY

Drawing upon past experiences to plan current lessons contributes to balancing the narrative and normative elements.

Intuiting an imbalance between the normative and the narrative creates opportunities for second chances to incorporate children's interests into future lessons.

Recognizing that children's attention can take many forms supports narrative pedagogy.

their subject matter proved to be accurate. Rarely does learning hinge upon one lesson. I, like my students, need second chances.

Sometimes I underestimate how children pay attention and what they absorb. As I walked over to Ted, the fifth "*Star Wars*" boy (whose grandmother was the art therapist), he was happily playing with his museum. He had made his dad, Claude Monet, himself, and me for his puppet characters. Ted had been unhappy in the museum, but as he played with his characters, he seemed to have forgotten the negative aspect of the experience. He was acting out my whole lesson plan script almost verbatim. It made me smile to see him imitate both Claude Monet and me and to watch how he and his dad walked inside the painting and described everything they saw. I felt relieved. My hunch was that the element of play that I hoped would engage the children when I first planned the lesson served to reconnect him.

CHAPTER 3

Art Class in the Museum

A FLOW EXPERIENCE

When children pretend, they aren't limited to the way things are in the real world. They're using their imaginations to move beyond the bounds of reality. A small child can be a powerful superhero, a crying baby, a mean dragon, or a scary lion—whatever he or she wants to be.

FRED ROGERS

PEDAGOGICAL CONSIDERATIONS

My most magical moment of teaching occurred the day I took a group of four and five-year-old children to see Robert Therrien's installation, *Under the Table*, at the Carnegie International Exhibit of Contemporary Art. It was our first class of the winter term of Art Express in the museum's Children's Studio. The theme was light and shadow. My co-teacher, Connie, and I had just finished our first activity of exploring the shapes of objects and their shadows on the overhead projector. I could sense that the children were feeling shy—even a little scared. Many of them were taking a class in the museum for the first time, some of them missing their parents. It was apparent to me that the "objects and their shadows" activity had not engaged them as I had hoped. Nevertheless, it was time to move from the studio classroom to the gallery.

For our gallery experience, Connie and I planned to have the children, armed with flashlights, explore light and shadows among Robert Therrien's giant 8 x 20-foot-long table and chairs. It seemed like an appropriate and playful way to explore this work of art in relation to our shadow theme. It reminded me of how I liked to construct tents as a child and play shadow games on the tent's surfaces with flashlights.

VIGNETTE—UNDER THE TABLE

Connie and I made our way to the top of the gallery stairs, flashlights in hand, with 22 preschoolers trailing behind us. I opened the door to the small gallery space that housed the gigantic, oversized table and chairs installation. To my surprise, I found the room crowded with very distinguished-looking adults, discussing the exhibit. I also noticed that the curator of the International was giving the famous talk known as The Curator's Tour to this group. I remembered that this curator strongly disliked children's art classes in the galleries. "Uh-oh," was my first response. "We better enter quietly."

I turned around to motion, "Shhhh!" and to say, "Let's tiptoe!" to the children, when suddenly, my 22 preschoolers, ignoring my gestures, scampered past me, fell down on their hands and knees, and meowed loudly like kittens. My eyes widened as I gave Connie the "Oh, no! What do we do now?" look. Then, without a second thought, I, too, spontaneously dropped down on my hands and knees and crawled under the table. Adopting the role of the mother cat, I began to quietly meow and gestured with my "paws" for them to stay close to me. Within seconds, Connie joined us, taking on the role of the father cat. Without saying a word to each other, we abandoned our light and shadows lesson plan and followed the children's lead in play.

The on-looking adults and curator eyed this spectacle with surprise and curiosity. I realized that we were no longer an art class visiting a piece of installation art—we **became** part of the installation. I also realized that unlike the adults who observed the installation from a distance and objectively commented, "This must be what it feels like to be my cat," the children **became** the cats.

In the next few minutes, a story line to our play evolved. Connie and I were the protective parent cats, the children were our hungry baby kittens, and the by-standing adults and curator were the scary giants who lived in the house with the big table and chairs. I encouraged my hungry babies to crawl out of my lap and venture out to gather imaginary crumbs of food off the floor left by the giants. One by one, the children carefully crept away from me to the edges of the table, purring and meowing. Upon seeing the legs and feet of the on-looking adults, the children scampered back to my lap for safety. They repeated this play theme to what seemed to be their endless enjoyment. I felt as if time stood still, and all I could sense was being present to the children. The children's pleasure and level of engagement was high. We could have continued this activity for hours. But announcing a time when the giants had fallen asleep, we scurried out of the gallery on our four paws and meowed our way down the stairs to the safe haven of the Children's Studio.

The excitement remained high as the children began their new activity. No one seemed to miss his or her parents anymore. When class was over and their parents came to pick them up, the children could not stop talking about the gigantic table and chairs. One by one, they dragged their parents to visit the installation. Without consciously planning it, by responding to the children's make-believe play, Connie and I had tapped into what was really on some of their minds—their fears around being in a new place without their parents.

BALANCING SENSIBILITIES

After all of the children had been picked up, I looked at Connie in total amazement. I had never thought the lesson would take this imaginative turn. I had to laugh. It happened at a time when we were being watched by the most distinguished group of visitors. It was interesting that although I knew we were the object of their curiosity, I felt unconcerned about their astonished gazes. Somehow their presence no longer mattered as I was caught up in the moment with the children, doing what felt right. I could sense the children's intense pleasure. I, too, felt exhilarated. It was one of those lessons where everything seemed to flow. I had that really great feeling that I get when I know the children have had a meaningful and powerful experience. In short, I experienced flow, which Csikszentmihalyi and Hermanson describe as "a state of mind that [is] spontaneous, almost automatic like the flow of a strong current." They go on to say, that individuals experiencing flow express themselves without fear or embarrassment; they feel unselfconscious, joyful, and serene:

> One's mind and body become completely involved in the activity. Attention is focused and concentration is so intense that there is no attention left over to think about anything irrelevant or to worry about problems. In the flow state, a person is unaware of fatigue and the passing of time; hours pass by in what seems like minutes. The depth of enjoyment is enjoyable and intrinsically rewarding. In many cases, individuals describe the experience as becoming "one" with the environment—the painting, the music, the team.[1]

Csikszentmihalyi and Hermanson caution that individuals will have difficulty entering into flow "if they are concentrating too much on doing the right thing...if they feel intimidated...if they are worried about their performance...if a negative mental state prevails...if they are feeling afraid or incompetent...[or] if they are feeling self-conscious." Certainly, in *In Front of the Monet,* my concentration on performance and fear of looking incompetent undermined the conditions needed for flow.

---

1 Mihaly Csikszentmihalyi and Kim Hermanson, "Intrinsic Motivation in Museums: Why does one want to learn?" in *Public Institutions for Personal Learning: Establishing a Research Agenda,* eds. John H. Falk and Lynn D. Dierking (Washington, DC: American Association of Museums, 1995), 70.

In *Under the Table*, however, I had the sense of being fully alive to the children in the moment. I could have played our theme of mother cat and kitten for hours. I sensed the deep enjoyment of entering the children's experience and connecting with their world of imagination.

Flow is akin to what Lous Heshusius calls a participatory mode of consciousness, which "involve[s] a somatic, nonverbal quality of attention that necessitate[s] letting go of the focus on self." It results from "the ability to temporarily let go of all preoccupation with self and move into a state of complete attention." It is a frame of mind where "the self-conscious 'I' disappear[s]" and where the individual lets go of "the notion of being-separate-and-in-charge altogether." A participatory mode of consciousness is "a 'total turning to' the other which led not to a loss of self but to a heightened feeling of aliveness and awareness."[2] One is open, receptive, and fully listening.

Unlike my painful self-consciousness during *In Front of the Monet,* in *Under the Table* the presence of the curator and a room full of distinguished guests did not shift my attention from the children. I remained attuned to their imaginative impulse to play and could no longer tell who was initiating and who was responding during our playfulness. Although as a teacher I did not relinquish my responsibilities, I had let go of the notion of being-separate-and-in-charge. We were one together sharing the play in a reciprocal relationship.

NARRATIVE SENSIBILITY

A Narrative Frame of Mind is conducive to a state of flow and operates when we are not hard on ourselves or judgmental about our own actions and ideas.

A state of flow allows for more finely tuned balance of normative and narrative forces.

Participatory consciousness is a form of *embodied knowing*, which is also referred to as intuition,[3] somatic knowing,[4] and tacit knowing.

2 Lous Heshusius "Freeing Ourselves from Objectivity: Managing Subjectivity or Turning toward a Participatory Mode of Consciousness," *Educational Researcher* 23, no. 3 (1994), 15-18.

3 Rudolf Arnheim, "The Double-edged Mind: Intuition and the Intellect," in *Learning and Teaching the Ways of Knowing* ed. Elliot W. Eisner (Chicago, IL: University of Chicago Press, 1985).

4 Lous Heshusius and Keith Ballard, eds. *From Positivism to Interpretivism and Beyond* (New York: Teachers College Press, 1996).

One has an instinctive feeling for what is working or not; it is what Nelson Goodman calls a "rightness" of fit.[5] Our bodies let us know when we are doing the right thing or going astray. In *Under the Table*, my rational thought would have cried out, "Warning!" as I looked around and saw the crowded room with the curator who disliked children's classes in the galleries. Instead, following my intuition, I spontaneously dropped to my hands and knees.

In *Teachers' Everyday Use of Imagination and Intuition*, Virginia Jagla wrote:

> In the vernacular, intuitions were often referred to as "hunches," "instincts," "gut feelings" or "guesses." As a form of action, to intuit was replaced by verbs as "to see," "to know," "to sense," "to perceive," or "to feel." Often these words were preceded by the word "just." "I just knew," "it just felt right," "I just sensed that," thus, meaning, "It is nothing more than that," or "I cannot explain it any further." The sensations or feelings related to intuition are often sensed within one's body. Consequently, we have expressions such as "I feel it in my bones," "I know it in my heart," or "it was a gut reaction." ...Intuition is something you instinctively feel inside yourself.[6]

Informed intuition or tacit knowledge is "a way to know more than we can tell." It is knowledge incorporated into our bodies; knowledge gained as we extend our bodies to include it; knowledge we come to dwell within.[7] For instance, I had played the cat and mother game with young children when I taught at the school for blind children and recalled in my journal:

NARRATIVE SENSIBILITY

Informed intuition, tacit knowledge, and embodied memories help us respond with "rightness of fit" within pedagogical moments.

---

5   Nelson Goodman, *Ways of Worldmaking* (Indianapolis, IN: Hackett Publishing Co., 1978), 138.
6   Virginia M. Jagla, *Teachers' Everyday Use of Imagination and Intuition* (New York: State University of New York Press, 1994), 34.
7   Michael Polanyi. *The Tacit Dimension* (London: Routledge and Kegan Paul, 1967).

It seems that embedded in my body are memories of
past pleasurable learning experiences with children.
I remember the feelings. When I was under the table,
and I began to sense their joy and mine, it was as if
subconsciously I was saying, "Hey, I've felt this before.
This is what it feels like when I connect. And that's why
I continued to follow those feelings. I just knew.

Over time I have internalized both personal and professional experiences that have gone well or not. I respond out of those memories embedded in my body. Also stored within my body are pleasurable childhood feelings about play and making art, which contributed to the magical feeling of the lesson. Edith Cobb[8] wrote that as adults our early experiences of play and wonder are awakened in us when we use our imaginations.

Even though in *Under the Table*, I did not reach my specific normative goal of exploring light and shadows with the flashlights, I accomplished a broader narrative aim for children to have a deeply pleasurable experience with a work of art. As Csikszentmihalyi and Hermanson might say, I created a greater opportunity for the children to enter flow, which is more likely to happen when the learner is intrinsically motivated. "When playing, children pay attention because they want to, because they find the information interesting and important in its own right."[9]

What informed my intuition that helped me to respond in a narrative frame of mind in *Under the Table*? One intuition was that many of the children were experiencing some anxiety about being separated from their parents in the museum for the first time. By joining in the children's imaginary play, I offered them an opportunity to explore their feelings. Possibly the scary giants represented their fears, and I was the surrogate parent providing a safe lap for the kittens. They could come back and forth to safety as they repeatedly ventured out into the scary world of the museum and giants beyond the edges of the table.

---

8   Edith Cobb, *The Ecology of Imagination in Childhood* (Dallas, TX: Spring Publications, 1977).
9   Csikszentmihalyi and Hermanson, 68.

Another tacit understanding was the importance of giving children opportunities to respond to works of art in ways that "fit" their developmental age. Colbert[10] and Kerlavage[11] underscore the importance of play or storytelling as modalities through which children incorporate the meaning of experiences. More than a year later, I visited an exhibit of Robert Therrien's work in Boston. The curator's wall text explained that the exhibit's giant door with a keyhole and a stack of plates piled high tapped into Therrien's childhood memories and world of make-believe. I wanted to write a letter telling him how my four- and five-year-old's inclination to play under the table allowed them to "get" his art in their own way. I think he would have loved knowing that the children became the cats, while the adults stood around merely saying, "This is what it must feel like to be my cat."

The children's kinesthetic, emotional, and playful responses revealed their interpretation that Therrien had created an imaginary play world for pets and little people. They were at home under his gigantic table, because they had spent the first four years of their lives crawling and standing up under tables in their own homes. In a sense, they embodied the interpretation as they dramatized it through play.

NARRATIVE SENSIBILITY

Understanding child development and the role of play in children's learning helps to create pleasurable aesthetic learning experiences.

An aesthetic experience, according to John Dewey, involves both the acts of perception and enjoyment. Knowing that many of the children took their parents back to see *Under the Table*, my sense was that encountering this work of art was both pleasurable and memorable. About an individual's relationship with a work of art, Dewey wrote:

---

10 Cynthia B. Colbert, "Developmentally Appropriate Practice in Early Art Education," in *The Visual Arts and Early Childhood Learning,* ed. Christine M. Thompson. Reston, VA: National Art Education Association, 1995, 35-39.

11 Marianne Kerlavage, "A Bunch of Naked Ladies and a Tiger: Children's Responses to Adult Works of Art," in *The Visual Arts and Early Childhood Learning,* ed. Christine M. Thompson (Reston, VA: National Art Education Association, 1995), 56-62.

> A work of art, no matter how old or classic, is actually not just potentially, a work of art only when it lives in some individual experience. A piece of parchment, of marble, of canvas, it remains...self-identical throughout the ages. But as a work of art, it is re-created every time it is aesthetically experienced. [12]

I would like to think that, in a way that was unique to their development, many of the children had Dewey's "aesthetic experience."

When I plan well, I have greater freedom to depart from my plan. I can go with the flow, because my attention can be on the children and not on the logistics of a lesson. Improvisation is, as dance educator Susan Stinson wrote, "creating movement as one goes along." In improvisation:

> The responsibility of the participants is to be open to the movement that develops, rather than trying to control it or make it go in a predetermined direction, and to stay constantly aware of and sensitive to other participants. The structure provides boundaries but within those one expects surprises and discoveries. Sometimes even the boundaries change. Improvisation seemed to me then, as it does now, an apt metaphor for a process in which teachers and children engage together with mutual respect, and lesson plans provide only a structure within which all participants can make meaningful discoveries. [13]

Under the Table illustrated the power of improvisational teaching. The lesson plan provided the initial boundaries, but the boundaries were free to change without

NARRATIVE SENSIBILITY

Planning well allows for improvisation.

---

12 John Dewey, *Art as Experience* (New York: Putnam, 1934), 108.

13 Susan Stinson, Dance as Curriculum, Curriculum as Dance, in *Reflections from the Heart of Educational Inquiry: Understanding Curriculum and Teaching through the Arts,* eds. George Willis and William H. Schubert, (Albany, New York: State University of New York Press, 1991). 191-192

resulting in chaos. Within the structure, surprises and discoveries arose as we created our own cat and kitten drama. The lesson was rich in reciprocity—that mutual respect that Stinson refers to—as the children and the teachers followed each other's lead.

CHAPTER 4

Aesthetics in the Art Classroom as Studio

"WHOSE ART IS IT ANYWAY?"

I propose that, as we share with our students what we think is meaningful, true, and beautiful, we must also listen to what our students experience as meaningful, true, and beautiful. We must also carefully listen to how they <u>process</u> what we think is meaningful, true, and beautiful. This model expands our concept of the role of teacher to that of listener and learner. It stresses the importance of identifying and respecting many forms of aesthetic experience. This model of education requires reciprocation and interaction. At its best, it is a dynamic relationship.

GRACE DENISTON-TROCHTA[1]

---

1 Grace Deniston-Trochta," The Meaning of Storytelling as Pedagogy," *Visual Arts Research 24*, no. 2 (1998), 31.

PEDAGOGICAL CONSIDERATIONS

The art classroom as studio is a place where children can be *originators* or *creators* of visual images and forms. It is a place where young children can learn to communicate and express a personal vision through visual representations.[2] Among my normative aims are supporting children's explorations of subject matter and development of images that are personally meaningful[3] as giving them "a reason for making art."[4]

Although I value listening in a narrative frame of mind, sometimes the children's subject matter troubles me. Is the subject matter too violent, crude, or stereotypical? Do the pressures of media and popular culture on young children subvert their authentic artmaking? In the following vignette, I share an instance when these normative issues overwhelmed my capacity to hear the children's narratives, and how listening to their narratives changed my perception of what is appropriate art making.

The following vignette took place with older primary-age children and refers to an art project where the children made puppets of a favorite pet. Because the children had been studying architecture with their homeroom teacher, I decided to build upon this interest by having them draw puppet stages. I gave the children a lot of freedom in their choice of imagery—or so I thought.

VIGNETTE—
POKEMON™ INVADES THE CLASSROOM

Pedagogical Enactment—Part 1

Michael, a very advanced drawer for an eight-year-old, had already spent hours carefully rendering columns, auditorium, curtains, chairs for the audience, ticket counters, dressing rooms, refreshment

---

2   See Martin Buber, 1965; Marilyn Zurmuehlen, 1990; Edith Gwathmey and Ann-Marie Mott, 2000. (Full citations in Bibliography)
3   Smith, 1983.
4   Jo Alice Leeds, "Teaching and the Reasons for Making Art," *Art Education 39*, no. 4 (1986): 17.

counters—any architectural feature that would make his puppet stage special. When Michael and a group of boys asked if they could go out in the hallway to finish drawing their stages, I said, "Fine."

When I checked on their progress 15 minutes later, they were engaged in animated conversation about their images—just the type of cooperation and collaboration I valued. Then I looked at their work and was shocked. Michael had drawn hundreds of strange, cartoon-like characters over the front of his beautifully rendered stage. I looked at the other boys' drawings; these too, were covered with odd, stereotypical cartoon characters.

"Michael, what are you drawing?" I asked incredulously, unable to conceal my disappointment.

"Oh, we're drawing Pokemon," he said and proceeded to introduce the different characters.

Completely oblivious to my disappointment, he returned to his drawing. His friends admired Michael's work, and his pride was visible as the others asked him how to draw their favorite Pokemon™ characters.

It was a little too late to do anything about the invasion of Pokemon™ characters into the safe enclave of the art classroom. The children's projects had been drawn with permanent marker, so I would never ask them to redo their stages. Yet, from my biased, adult aesthetic viewpoint, this was not what children's art should look like.

Pedagogical Enactment—Part 2

After the children had completed their stages and performed their puppet shows, we moved on to our next art project, creating illustrated books about our puppets. Their stories could be biographical—a history of how their puppet came to be—or a mystery, a romance, an adventure story, or a comedy. Right when the children were on the edges of their seats in anticipation ready to begin, I declared, "Oh, by the way, there will not be any Pokemon drawings in this project!"

"What? No Pokemon!" A few of the children exclaimed.

"That's right. Besides, that's what your sketchbooks are for. You can draw as many Pokemon drawings as you want in them."

As the children began to create their puppet biographies, I observed a surge of imagination and enthusiasm. None of them seemed to be at a loss for ideas—and all of them seemed to be deeply engaged. As I looked at their books, I was amazed at their humor and originality. I could sense how good they felt about themselves and what they had created. Michael had created an adventure biography about his pet dog becoming a famous detective.

It seemed I had made the right decision to exclude Pokemon™. Yet, as I watched their work unfold, I felt a twinge of guilt. Had I done the right thing in censoring Pokemon™? Didn't I want them to have ownership of their ideas? Didn't I want to encourage free expression? Didn't I want the children to be the originators of their work—even if they borrowed images from popular culture? Whose art is it anyway?

BALANCING SENSIBILITIES

John Dewey maintained, "Until we understand, we are, if we have curiosity, troubled, baffled, and hence moved to inquire."[5] Missing in this situation was any desire to *understand* what Pokemon™ *meant* to Michael and his friends. I was not *moved* to inquire. I had no curiosity to turn on the television, rent the movie videos, or even sit down with the children to hear why the characters were so captivating. My mind and spirit were closed—I did not like the characters' physical appearances, nor did I like the inclusion of these cartoon-like images in the children's artmaking. As I result, I automatically censored them.

Max van Manen contends that teachers need a sensibility of *nonjudgmental understanding*, which "involve[s] a listening that [is] receptive, open, sympathetic, authentic, and facilitative":

> To children it may often appear that even when adults ask them about their experience, the adults are not really interested in listening to them. For example, the adult asks, "Why did you do that?" or "What did you do that for?" But this question is rarely meant to provide an opportunity for the child to be heard. More often the

5   John Dewey, *How We Think* (New York: D. C. Heath & Co, 1933). 132.

adult has already made up his or her mind in judging the child. Often the "why" is meant to reprimand the child, even though the child's response—if only the adult would really listen—might make the adult more thoughtful and understanding about the child's world.[6]

Carlina Rinaldi, a pedagogical consultant to Reggio Children, stated that listening to children "requires a deep awareness and at the same time a suspension of our judgments and above all our prejudices; it requires openness to change." Listening welcomes differences and recognizes the value of other's point of view.[7] I certainly had not exhibited these sensibilities toward the children's narrative.

In understanding children and their point of view, William Ayers stated that teachers need to be one-part detective, one-part researcher, and one-part world-class puzzle master. We need to "sift the clues children leave, follow the leads, and diligently uncover the facts in order to fill out and make a credible story of their growth and development." Further, we need to "painstakingly [fit] together the tiny pieces of some mammoth, intricate jigsaw of childhood."[8] Because children are always growing and changing, we need to continue to listen, ask why, and seek to understand.

Dewey suggested that when we quit wondering "why," it is usually because our curiosity has been blunted by routine. Maxine Greene stated that teachers need to cultivate the ability to "take a fresh look at the taken for granted…without that ability, most of us, along with our students, would remain submerged in the habitual."[9]

The "way we understand children is a telltale of the way we understand ourselves; we "truly open ourselves to the child's way of being when we are able to experience openness ourselves."[10] In other

---

6   van Manen, *The Tact of Teaching*, 86, 84.
7   Carlina Rinaldi, "Documentation and Assessment: What is the relationship?" in *Making Learning Visible: Children as Individual and Group Learners*, eds. Claudia M. Guidici, Mara Krechevsky and Carlina Rinaldi (Reggio Emilia, Italy: Reggio Children, 2001). 81.
8   William Ayers, *To Teach: The Journey of a Teacher* (New York: Teachers College Press, 1993). 33.
9   Maxine Greene, *Releasing the Imagination: Essays on Education, the Arts, and Social Change* (San Francisco, CA: Jossey-Bass, 1995), 100.
10 Max van Manen, *The Tone of Teaching* (Portsmouth, NH: Heinemann, 1986), 30.

words, if I want to be able to understand the child's point of view, I first needed to understand what keeps me from being open to their interests.

Part of me detested the Pokemon™ aesthetic for being too cartoonish, too unnatural—a feeling not uncommon to an art teacher who was trained to snub cartoons and other forms of popular culture. The Pokemon™ images stood out in sharp contrast to the beautifully rendered architectural detail in Michael's stage. The Pokemon™ figures had no relationship to his puppet character or play. From my narrow point of view, I felt that his drawing lacked the spontaneity and authenticity of his own personal style and mark-making.

Interestingly, many of my art teacher colleagues shared my aversion to Pokemon™ images and prohibited their inclusion in art class projects. When I asked for their reasons, they responded: "It was not authentic." "It was not original." "Their images were not their own." When I asked them what they said to their children who wanted to include these images in their projects, they replied, "Other artists created these images. You want to create your own." "If you copy, you are not using your imagination. In art, we use our imagination."

Equally interesting was Antonio's response, when I asked how he resolved the Pokemon™ dilemma in his K-4 public school classes. I was taken aback when he responded, "What dilemma?" Antonio, who was in his twenties, loved popular culture and borrowed images from it for his own artwork. In one lesson he even used Pokemon™ to connect children to Andrew Wyeth's painting of *Christina's World*. After explaining that Christina was lying in the foreground of the picture, and she was paralyzed, Antonio pulled a Pokeball out of his pocket and asked, "If you could create your own Pokemon character with special powers to give to Christina, what would you create and what special powers would it have?" The children were enthralled and, at the same time, learned about a painting that they would encounter again. Unlike me, Antonio was able to connect their narrative to his normative aim—which was having a meaningful encounter with a work of art.

My education about Pokemon™ continued one Thursday evening when I happened upon a Pokemon™ club that met weekly in the children's section of a bookstore. The store had capitalized on the children's interests and designed all sorts of activities where they could trade cards and play games. Although I knew it was a marketing ploy,

I could not deny the enthusiasm and the pleasure the children derived from playing Pokemon™. I decided to take some of their drawing activities back to school with me. One day after the children finished their art projects, I said, "If you want to, you can draw your favorite Pokemon characters or make them in clay." Daniel, who had little interest in learning to draw (and as a result tended to disrupt the class), immediately jumped at the opportunity.

The following morning as I was setting up for class, Daniel's father made a special trip to visit me. He told me all Daniel could do these days was draw Pokemon™ characters. In the past, Daniel had little interest in art. "Now I think we have found the thing that we have been looking for to make the connection. We need to capitalize on this." Although I shuddered inside at his use of the marketing metaphor, I, too, rejoiced that Daniel had found something that he loved to draw.

As I continued to explore my reasons for detesting the Pokemon™ aesthetic, I thought back to my undergraduate education. In the late 1970s, the prevailing theories regarded children's artistic development as predictable and unchanging regardless of context or culture.[11] Too much exposure and reliance on media-dominated images was thought "to curtail youngsters' own imaginative efforts, and in the absence of any pedagogical intervention, to cut them adrift from the larger world of aesthetic understanding."[12] I had learned to support children's predictable unfolding development by connecting their artmaking primarily to experiences within home and family.

Curiously, despite this early training, I had grown to embrace images borrowed from the media and popular culture. When children drew scenes from *Star Wars*, *Harry Potter*, *Little Mermaid*, or *Ninja Turtles*, their imagery did not offend my adult concept of child art. I believed children could render these characters *in their own style* of drawing the human figure or animals. Furthermore, I strongly believed that children needed a place to freely draw whatever they wanted. For many children, drawing Darth Vader and other images from popular culture in their sketchbooks gave them a reason to make art. Drawing

---

11 Patricia Tarr, "Reflections on the Image of the Child: Reproducer of Culture or Creator of Culture," *Art Education 56, no.* 4 (2003): 6-11.

12 Judith M. Burton, "The Configuration of Meaning: Learner-centered Art Education Revisited." *Studies in Art Education* 41, no. 4 (2000): 332.

with their friends and sharing ideas and tricks and techniques—e.g., how to render a perfect Ninja turtle or how to draw a tyrannosaurus rex—could become an avenue for learning how to draw.

So why did the cartoon-like Pokemon™ aesthetic offend me, even when I was open to children's use of other images from popular culture? First, the cartoon-like images clashed with my notion of the natural unfolding of young children's artmaking. Cartoons belonged to adults and to their older peers. In fact, I included projects around cartooning with my middle school students, because I saw this as an avenue for humor, creativity, and social commentary. However, I wanted to protect the youngest children for as long as possible from these cultural influences. I did not like the way adults in early childhood settings filled the environment with "cute, smiling cartoon figures decorating walls and sugarcoating worksheets."[13]

Second, over the years I had seen some children feel safe only when drawing cartoons, happy faces, or stick figures. When drawing a self-portrait while looking in a mirror, or drawing a pet from life, some reverted to cartoon schema instead of using all of their senses to closely observe the object in front of them. Because I believe that drawing is a way of coming to know—about self, others, and the larger world—it is important that children become fluent in their ability to draw, just as they are fluent in reading or writing. I want them to go beyond facile stereotypes and move into the realm of the personal and the imaginative. Cartoon-like images could derail the natural unfolding of artistic activity.

Third, Pokemon™ epitomized for me media manipulation and commercialism, reducing children to pawns in a larger-than-life marketing scheme. By censoring Pokemon™, I naively felt I was protecting the children from negative cultural influences. Again, I was not alone in my thinking. In her article, "Kinderculture in the Art Classroom," Thompson stated that many art teachers had difficulty with the ideological underpinnings of media-inspired images, which too often reflected "physical aggression, gender stereotypes, and improbable relations between cause and effect." She continued:

---

13 Tarr, 7.

> Not only do many adults find it impossible to discern the value of learning to draw a Pokeball or Pikachu or the Little Mermaid; in some cases, we shudder to think that, along with the cuddly affectionate sea creatures and the do-or-die mentality, young children are passively absorbing the less savory messages these characters convey. At best, we think there are better things for children to do with their time. At worst, we worry that they are inhaling hazardous materials as they teach themselves to draw Ariel or Jiggly Puff.[14]

Thompson challenged early art educators to re-assess their developmental and cultural assumptions about children and the role of popular culture in their artmaking. The world of childhood has changed since my undergraduate art education. Then, prevailing traditions focused on the solitary child living in a unified world. The world was their backyard; images were largely autobiographical, drawn from their direct experiences with family and neighborhood friends.

Now, the world of childhood has widened to include "films, television programs and advertising, student and youth clubs, church and social groups, sports, comic books, trading cards, computer games, the Internet, and so forth."[15] They have access to more unfiltered media information and are exposed to a wider range of people, ideas, and images. In her study of contemporary children's drawings, when asked to draw whatever they wanted, Thompson noted that although the autobiographical images were not completely absent, "they were rare enough to stand out rather starkly amid other drawings of Pokemon™ characters, dinosaurs, space ships, and the *Little Mermaid.*"[16] As children develop beyond the preschool and kindergarten years, many participate in a "kids only" world of popular culture set apart from the world of adults. In a sense, they develop their own aesthetic. In my art classes, many of my students, even in the kindergarten years—if not younger—construct their own aesthetic. Thompson explained:

---

14 Christine M. Thompson, Kinderculture in the Art Classroom: Early Childhood Art and the Mediation of Culture *Studies in Art Education* 44, no. 2 (2003), 141.

15 Joe L. Kincheloe, Patrick Slattery, and Shirley R. Steinberg, *Contextualizing Teaching* (New York: Addison Wesley Longman, 2000).

16 Thompson, 138.

> There are premonitions of this aesthetic even in
> kindergarten, where having knowledge and expertise
> not shared by adults is highly desirable, and drawing
> subjects seldom acknowledged in the official
> curriculum is half the fun. Reversing the typical power
> structure in the classroom is surely part of the appeal
> of memorizing endless facts about dinosaurs or tank
> engines or Pokemon characters.[17]

When children are left to draw whatever they want, these cultural images prevail. When teachers control the subject matter of the curriculum, fewer cartoons and media-inspired images appear in the art classroom.

In my situation, I saw that as Michael drew Pokemon™ image after image, he dazzled his friends and won their admiration. His sense of who he was as a classroom artist—his developing artistic identity— was coming into being as he impressed his peers in the privacy of the hallway, away from my presence. They were developing their own aesthetic in what Joe Kincheloe refers to as "subversive kinderculture." I saw how important it was for him to develop his artistic voice in this context. It was not a surprise that the following semester I had set up a drawing corner just for drawing their favorite Pokemon™ imagery, and I boldly displayed their work.

In *Popular Culture: Schooling and Everyday Life*, Giroux and Simon state that teachers need to understand the important role popular culture plays in students' growing identity and interest in schooling:

> Popular culture is appropriated by students and is
> a major source of knowledge for authorizing their
> voices and experiences, even as pedagogy authorizes
> the voices of the adult world of teachers and
> administrators.[18]

---

17 Thompson, 142.
18 Henry A. Giroux and Roger I. Simon, eds. *Popular Culture, Schooling, and Everyday Life* (Massachusetts: Bergin & Garvey, 1989), 221.

Could it be that I was adhering to a romanticized concept of the child? As early childhood educators, Dahlberg, Moss, and Pence explain:

> This [romanticized] image of the child generates in adults a desire to shelter children from the corrupt surrounding world—violent, oppressive, commercialized, and exploitative—by constructing a form of environment in which the young child will be offered protection, continuity, and security.[19]

The philosophy in Reggio Emilia education views children as co-constructors of knowledge, identity, and culture. Children are seen as "having a voice of their own and should be listened to as a means of taking them seriously, involving them in democratic dialogue and decision-making…"[20] When children are co-constructors, it equalizes the power in the classroom whereby the teacher is not the only authority on the content of subject matter. Children do not "passively endure their experience" in the world, but become "active agents in their socialization, co-constructed with their peers."[21] They are in the world as it is today and are acted upon by that world—but they also act on it and make meaning of it.

Through my reflections I came to see I had been naïve to think I could protect the children from experiencing Pokemon™; to believe they would not be exposed to it and actively seek it out in other contexts. My assumptions about children and their aesthetic

NARRATIVE SENSIBILITY

Helping children to negotiate influences of popular culture and their evolving aesthetic is an important aspect of teaching in a narrative frame of mind.

interests limited my ability to listen to the narrative. My prejudices resulted in a lack of "sensitivity to what [was] best for each child, having a sense of each child's life and his or her deep preoccupations."[22] Popular

---

19 Gunilla Dahlberg, Peter Moss, and Alan Pence, *Beyond Quality in Early Childhood Education and Care: Postmodern Perspectives* (Philadelphia, PA: Falmer Press, 1999), 45.
20 Dahlberg, Moss, and Pence, 49.
21 Rinaldi, 105.
22 van Manen, *Tone of Teaching*, 46.

culture, children's innate and
evolving aesthetic capacity, and
my own aesthetic values did
not need to be in conflict, if, in
a narrative frame of mind, I was
able to navigate among these
pedagogical forces.

**NARRATIVE
SENSIBILITY**

Self-awareness and self-
understanding can curtail
the forces that blunt open
curiosity.

Art educator Brent Wilson[23] suggests that respecting children's
inclination to draw imagery from popular culture need not result in
creating a "Pokemon curriculum." In fact, that could be detrimental
as children need the freedom to participate in their own subversive
culture that distinguishes their identity from that of adults. Prohibiting
the drawing of certain images during class projects increases their
transgressive power and motivates children to draw them outside of
class. Wilson believes that the
official curriculum should be
dedicated to the content of art
education that children might not
be exposed to on their own.

**NARRATIVE
SENSIBILITY**

Transgressive art making and
a "subversive kinderculture"
separate from the formal
art curriculum help children
develop their own aesthetic
and interest in artmaking.

When I invited the children
to create their own Pokemon™
characters out of clay, Susie
walked up to me and said, "You
know, Ms. Krakowski, not
everyone loves Pokemon." Susie reminded me that children's interests
are idiosyncratic, and just because several children are being influenced
by Pokemon™ in the media, the appeal isn't necessarily universal. And
so, I have to be attuned to their unique, individual interests and provide
many learning spaces for every child to grow in their personal choice
of subject matter and artistic expression.

When I asked the children to create their own imagery for their
pet biographies, their imaginations flourished; they were engaged
in the creative process, and expressed a sense of ownership of their
book. Finding a balance between free choice—the narrative—within
the normative parameters of the imagery for the art lesson proved to

---

23 Brent Wilson, *Manga, the Japanese Curriculum.* Paper presented at the National Art Education
    Association National Convention, Miami Beach, Florida, 2000.

be "educative" in this situation.[24] Michael continued to inspire his classmates when he drew his pet as a detective. He and his friends came into the after-school studio on their own time and created a series of books related to the life of their pets. It seemed that placing some parameters on the subject matter pushed them to discover new directions that they may not have explored otherwise. I saw that those limits, in moderation, could be useful.

> **NARRATIVE SENSIBILITY**
>
> Maintaining a narrative frame of mind entails balancing my interests with the children's interests and balancing varied interests among children.

Although I wished that in the situation with Michael and his friends their interest in Pokemon™ would have just gone away, I realized I had another option. I could let go of my adult notion of appropriate subject matter and explore new possibilities. I could begin to listen to the children's interests and welcome them into the classroom for the children to grow in meaningful artmaking, Thompson states that teachers need to consider creating a space for the children's interests in popular culture within the art classroom:

The nature and meaning of children's experiences—their interests, their concerns, their ways of thinking about the world and its representations—are obscured when adults confine children's attention to subject matter that reflects adult conceptions of the interests proper to childhood, rather than opening a space in which the true interests of contemporary children can emerge.[25]

Realizing that I was offering little space for the children's interests in the official curriculum, I began to consider different ways of responding. Katherine, a colleague, filled her classroom with children's toys and artifacts, such as dinosaurs, animals, action figures, and dolls. Many of her

> **NARRATIVE SENSIBILITY**
>
> Reciprocity between the art teacher's aesthetic interests and those of the children flattens power differentials in the classroom and promotes cooperative learning.

---

24 Dewey, *Education and Experience*, 25.
25 Thompson, "Kinderculture in the Art Classroom," 144-145.

projects were inspired by the children's interests. She told me that drawing Pokemon™ characters was a great way to teach children how to draw. Through the simplified shapes of the characters, children can see how to take a complicated object and break it down into simple basic shapes. She also told me that she collected her own Pokemon™ trading cards and at lunchtime traded them with interested children. For Katherine, listening to her children's narrative provided a way to connect and build a relationship with them while teaching them valuable drawing skills (her normative aim) in a way that appealed to them. I was reminded of what Basil Bernstein said, "If the culture of the teacher is to become part of the consciousness of the child, then the culture of the child must first be in the consciousness of the teacher."[26]

---

26 Basil Bernstein, "A Critique of the Concept "Compensatory Education," in *Functions of Language in the Classroom*, eds. Courtney B. Cazden, Vera P. John, and Dell Hymes (New York: Teachers College Press, 1972), 149.

CHAPTER 5

Aesthetics in the Art Classroom as Studio

"YOU HAVE THE FREEDOM TO CREATE WHATEVER YOU WANT"

*The classroom has all the elements of theater, and
the observant, self-examining teacher will not need a
drama critic to uncover character, ploy, and meaning.
We are, all of us, the actors trying to find the meaning
of the scenes in which we find ourselves.*

VIVIAN PALEY

PEDAGOGICAL CONSIDERATIONS

The following vignette takes place in the after-school art studio as three boys work on a skit for a puppet show that will be performed the following week in the art classroom.

In the past, this puppet project had been one of the children's favorites. I had adapted it from Jody Shell's lesson when she taught it to first and second grade children at the Carnegie Museum during their exhibit on the art of William Wegman. The children dressed their pet puppets like the dogs in the displayed William Wegman's books, Cinderella and Little Red Riding Hood, and then performed traditional or original fairy tales.

This particular year, however, some of the children said they did not want to perform fairy tales. In response, I gave them the freedom to write or adapt whatever story they wanted. I was curious to see what they would come up with on their own. Naively, when I gave them permission to create whatever they wanted, it did not cross my mind that any questionable subject matter would arise.

VIGNETTE—FIREMEN TO THE RESCUE

Just a few minutes after I walked into the after-school art studio, Chris motioned to me to come and see his group's latest idea for next week's puppet show. Bobby, Paul, and he had been laughing very hard. They had placed little white handmade surgical-like masks over the faces of their pet animal puppets. Now there's an intriguing notion, I thought, a puppet—which, in a sense, is already a persona—wearing a mask—which, in a sense, could be a new persona. The boys laughed again, interrupting my thinking.

I turned my attention to their performance already in progress and tried to make sense of what was happening. It looked as if Chris's puppet, a gerbil—and part detective—had received a phone call about a mysterious gas leak. He and his other pet friends—who looked like they could be firefighters—seemed to be on a mission to locate it.

When the puppets arrived on the scene of the gas leak, the gerbil and his friends began to faint. "Help! Help!" they cried. "We're being gassed out." They barged into the suspect's house and found their arch-enemy—the gray striped cat—sitting in the chair, passing gas. "Oh, no, it's a false alarm, it's not a gas leak, it's—it's that old cat—AND HE'S FARTING!" The boys then began to produce endless variations of flatulence. "Quick, boys, get your gas masks on again," commanded the gerbil. Immediately the three boys put the little white masks over their puppets' noses and frantically ran back and forth, trying to eradicate the smell.

I laughed at the sight of their puppets running around with their gas masks. Sensing that I found their skit humorous, the boys turned to me and announced, "It's our idea for next week's puppet show."

> "Oh?" I wasn't sure what to say. For an instant, I imagined their whole class running around the school making all sorts of unpleasant sounds with their puppets.
>
> "I don't think this would be an appropriate skit for the whole class," I responded.
>
> "Oh, please, please, pleeeeeeease," the boys begged me to reconsider.
>
> "I know that you can come up with another skit for the puppet show. You all have great imaginations."

The boys sensed that I wasn't going to budge. Although they were disappointed, Bobby and Paul seemed to be okay with my decision. On the other hand, Chris was not very happy, which took me by surprise, because we had a very good teacher-student relationship. I felt a twinge of guilt when I saw the anger in his face. These boys are incredibly creative, I rationalized to myself. I can't imagine them having a problem coming up with a new skit.

The following week the boys performed their newly created skit for the whole class. As I watched their halfhearted performance, I saw that it lacked the humor, spontaneity, and creativity that had been so evident in their after-school puppet show. I asked myself, "If I had to do it over again, would I let them perform their original skit?" I quickly dismissed the thought and turned my attention to the next group of students taking the stage. As I watched a modern-day version of Rapunzel performed by pet puppets, the look of disappointment on Chris' face lingered. Was he still angry at me? My feelings of uncertainty returned. Had I taken the right action in censoring the boys' after-school puppet show?

BALANCING SENSIBILITIES

During a conversation with Janet, an art education colleague, I shared with her the story about Chris and his friends. When I got to the part about the gas masks, Janet began to laugh, "What a great skit! I would have never censored it." I cringed when she used the word censor because it dawned on me that was what I had done.

"You wouldn't?" I asked.

"Are you kidding?" she responded incredulously.

Feeling defensive, I said, "You would have to understand this group. It's not the kind of class that I want to get out of control." Yet, after leaving our conversation, I thought, "Maybe Janet was right. Maybe I should have been more open-minded and flexible." I was uncomfortable with the idea that I had "censored" the boys, and I was sorry I had angered Chris. On the other hand, I told myself, "No, I'm not sure if this felt right. I'm not sure that I would have felt comfortable allowing their skit with the bathroom humor to be presented to the whole class."

My growing guilt and uncertainty motivated me to call Darla, a close colleague, with whom I had worked for eleven years at the school for blind children. Frequently I went to Darla whenever I encountered issues or concerns related to children's emotional development. She is a play therapist, working from a psychoanalytical perspective. Over the years, she has helped me think through challenging situations. I was convinced that she would tell me that I was repressing the children's natural desire to put on a bathroom skit.

I was surprised when Darla began talking about public and private space and how we are living in a culture with no clear boundaries between the two. Swearing, talking about sex, bathroom talk, and other people's music blaring are all "out there" to be heard whether we want to or not. Children are constantly being exposed to interests and conversations through media that had once been reserved for adult-only viewing. Darla wondered if the blurring of boundaries results in less *civility*. As adults, she suggested, we need to help children know the difference.

I could relate to what Darla was saying, picturing a few of my students who were having difficulty knowing the difference—or knew the difference and seemed not to care. I thought of one preschooler, John, who came to school for the kindergarten visitation day. During these visits, it is customary for the teachers to take a Polaroid snapshot of the children in small groups. When the picture of John's group came out of the camera, he was giving the middle finger to the camera.

A few years later, after another incident when he was in second grade, I wrote about John in my teacher journal:

> *In front of the video recorder and his female classmates, John announced the name of his imaginary animal. "This is Butt Baby Girl." I responded by asking him to come up with different name.*

Repeatedly I found myself talking with John, particularly about his interactions and comments with many of the girls. At times it was exhausting. His classroom teacher found this to be the case as well.

I thought of another situation, in which I had taken a group of middle school children on a field trip to a contemporary art museum. Because we were a large group, we divided into two smaller groups for our tour. On the day of the field trip one of the classroom teachers who had planned to accompany me became ill, so he sent his student teacher. I had to keep reminding a few boys in my group to respond appropriately—something that caused me some embarrassment. When the tour was over, and we met the other group, I saw that the student teacher was almost in tears. A large part of her group had responded so inappropriately that the tour guide was almost in tears, too. I wanted to crawl into a hole and hide. When I thought about some of these students who had acted disrespectfully, I recalled repeated instances from their intermediate years (many of them had transferred from other schools where they were also having difficulty) when they seemed to be insensitive to the feelings of others around them—both adults and children. Now as teenagers, they were displaying a similar lack of sensitivity and respect. On some level, I could identify with this notion of the public and private space.

I said to Darla, "So much seems to be related to age and context." I then shared with her a situation that I had written about in my journal concerning a group of kindergarteners' first experience with brown earthenware clay. This situation occurred in what Darla and I were calling public space—the daily classroom.

> *I sat down next to Nate who was immersed in rolling long coils of clay. Suddenly he had a burst of insight and turned to me, exclaiming what he believed to be the most obvious thing in the world, "Hey! This looks like poop!" I looked at his small clay creations he made and said, "You're right, it does."*

"Darla," I said, "I would never censor a comment like the one Nate made." "Yes," Darla replied, "It is so much where he was developmentally—he is only a few years out of potty training. I don't believe that young children should be shamed for making natural observations such as Nate's." I agreed, which is why I had not censored him.

Then another kindergarten "first" experience with clay came to mind. The children were making winter animal homes for little plastic toy woodland animals using earthenware clay and natural materials. In wanting to nurture a sense of empathy on the part of the children toward our school's backyard animals, I asked the class to work in pairs and create a warm and comfortable home that would keep the animal safe from the cold weather and from predators. Sarah and Mary called me over to show me their home.

> Do you see this little TV screen here? This is where the bear's mom and dad can see if any predators come to the door. And over here—this is where the baby bear sleeps. That's why we put all those soft leaves on it. And here's the kitchen. In this little bowl is the bear's food. And here's the toilet." Mary rolls away some pine needles and shows me little round pellets of clay in the toilet that she then covers up like kitty litter.

Sarah and Mary made me smile. I responded, "You're taking good care of your baby bear, aren't you? You've thought of everything she needs."

As Darla and I continued to talk, she reminded me of Jane Katch's book, Under Deadman's Skin.[1] Katch wrote about her five- and six-year-old students' fascination with violent fantasy play and how she and the students came to negotiate what felt safe in the classroom. Darla said, "Do you remember how she was able to talk to the children about how she was feeling uncomfortable about their violent play? In the process she came to a deeper understanding of what this play meant to the children and how together they re-negotiated the learning space."

"Instead of responding with a knee-jerk reaction," she continued, "you could have talked with them—or even the whole class—and explored their thinking on the subject. What were their thoughts on the difference between private and public appropriate subject matter? Who would be comfortable with certain subject matter? Who wouldn't? Why might we not want to do bathroom humor in public? What were your thoughts on this? Did you have any solution to this? Instead, there was no listening to their viewpoints, no conversation. Just as important, you could have explained to them that you were feeling uncomfortable with their skit and why. Since the skit evoked an immediate laugh from you, you could have talked about how they could take what was good about their play and rework that into a new play that was appropriate for public viewing."

"Darla's right," I thought, "Here was another instance where I closed down the listening space. If I had talked with the boys, possibly a different classroom narrative could have unfolded." Loris Malaguzzi[2] reminds teachers that it is through ongoing dialogue that children can understand our expectations, and we can understand theirs. I realized that dialogue was missing in my interactions with Chris and his friends as well as with Michael in the Pokemon™ situation in the previous chapter.

Isaacs wrote that the "heart of dialogue [is] a simple but profound capacity to listen."[3] It was about:

---

1   Jane Katch, *Under Deadman's Skin: Discovering the Meaning of Children's Violent Play* (Boston, MA: Beacon Press, 2001).
2   Loris Malaguzzi, "Your Image of the Child: Where Teaching Begins," *Child Care Information Exchange* 96 (1994): 52-56.
3   William Isaacs, *Dialogue and the Art of Thinking Together* (New York: Doubleday, 1999), 83.

[a] shared inquiry, a way of thinking and reflecting together. It was not something that you did to another person. It was something you did *with* people…[A] large part of learning this has to do with learning to shift your attitudes about relationships with others, so that we gradually give up the effort to make them understand us and come to a greater understanding of ourselves and each other.[4]

Art educator Lisa Schoenfielder learned that for genuine dialogue to occur in her classroom, she had to "hold on to one's side of the relationship and at the same time attempt to experience the other side."[5] In the process of trying to understand her students, she must be willing to being changed. Addressing the importance of mutuality and dialogue in the Reggio schools, Rinaldi described how the teachers create "a listening context"—a space "where one learns to listen and to narrate."[6] This context invites multiple listening, where each child, groups of children, and teachers all listen to each other and to themselves, overturning the traditional teaching-learning relationship.

Paulo Freire maintained that in a traditional teaching-learning relationship, the teacher views the child as a passive or empty vessel to be filled with knowledge. This creates an unequal distribution of power between the child and adult. Freire proposed an alternative—a mutual listening and telling, whereby the "teacher is no longer merely the one-who-teaches"[7] but is listening and learning alongside the students. If we are to have more democratic classrooms, then dialogue and mutual respect are essential.

I needed to be more open, nonjudgmental, and accepting of children's interest in popular culture and to create a space in the art studio for their "unofficial interests."[8] I realized that this did not answer all my questions or resolve the tension that existed in how I would deal

---

4   Isaacs, 9.
5   Lisa Schoenfielder, *Searching for the Shape of Content in a Studio Based Approach to Art Education* (Unpublished doctoral dissertation, University of Iowa, 1996), 43.
6   Rinaldi, "Documentation and Assessment: What is the relationship?", 89.
7   Paulo Freire, *Pedagogy of the Oppressed* (New York: Herder and Herder, 1970), 61.
8   Thompson, "Kinderculture in the Art Classroom,145.

with the issue of popular culture in all situations. In fact, my reflections generated more questions. Did listening to and welcoming the narrative always mean letting the children do whatever they wanted, whenever they wanted? What about children who drew only one subject and resisted trying anything new? Were there times when it was appropriate or in the children's best interest to limit or direct the subject matter?

In response to these questions, I realized that negotiating a balance between the children's powerful interests in popular culture and my normative aims requires an intuitive response that I refer to as, "it depends." In some of the situations I encounter there is no definitive right answer; however, there seems to be some more or less beneficial ways of responding. I need to look at each situation as unique, requiring an improvisational thoughtfulness and an openness to listening to the children. Each situation depends on the context, my knowledge of the students and their interests, my knowledge of the curriculum, and what direction would be most worthwhile at that time.

For example, at the beginning of each school year the children draw their self-portrait on the covers of their personal sketchbooks. I encourage them to observe their faces closely in the mirror and draw from observation. Usually, the children enjoy this activity.

NARRATIVE SENSIBILITY

Context matters when making decisions about what is and is not appropriate in children's art.

Maintaining a narrative frame of mind allows for wiser, less knee-jerk decisions regarding freedom and boundaries within the public and private space of art making.

Dialogue helps to see others' points of view.

One year, however, a new student who, instead of drawing from observation, drew a monster-like cartoon of himself on his sketchbook cover. Rather than intervene, I chose to step back and watch, sensing it was important to give him more latitude on this first day in a new school. I wanted him to feel comfortable and secure. Further, he excelled in drawing, and I wanted him to receive the approval of his classmates. Because I did not know him well enough to understand why he chose to draw the monster, I believed it was best to follow his lead. For the next three projects, although he resisted drawing anything but his fantasy monster characters, I continued to stand back. A few months into the school year, I met his mother who told me that Mark loved my art class. He had been home schooled for a while because he resisted trying new things in his former school. She thanked me for being willing to let him pursue his monster drawings even when the lesson had nothing to do with monsters.

If I had censored Mark, he might have turned inward. Intuition told me that he needed the freedom to draw his monsters. Because I won his trust and possibly respect, he began to participate in most of the projects. Together Mark and I negotiated ways for him to both try new things but still create his monsters when needed. He also faithfully came in during after-school hours to pursue his monster drawings with his friends and teach them his drawing strategies.

In the situation with Chris and the puppets, I was experiencing a tension between free expression and boundaries. I was so troubled because I value both. Van Manen wrote that the normative dimension of teaching gives rise to many of the contradictions and tensions of teaching. The contradictions we encounter, he suggested, are a result of the tensions between contrasting principles, such as, "freedom versus control, security versus risk, self versus other, right versus wrong, real versus ideal, the interest of the person versus the interest of society, and so on."[9] A good example that surfaces in teaching, he said, is the tension between freedom and control. For example, children need both freedom and order, and an environment that is either too permissive or too authoritarian can be detrimental to children's growth. A pedagogical tension such as this, he said, challenges the teacher to reflect and respond thoughtfully. There is always never one right answer for all children. Each pedagogical situation is unique, and each pedagogical situation requires its own particular response.

When I shared the story of Chris with Doriane, another friend with a child development background, she echoed Darla's concern that our cultural boundaries between private and public spaces have been greatly dissolved, leaving children with a confused sense of self. Appropriate boundaries are necessary for children to be able to function healthily in a culture as well as to develop a strong sense of self and identity. Her comments reminded me of the book, *Beyond Self-Esteem:*

---

9   van Manen, *The Tact of Teaching*, 61.

Developing a Genuine Sense of Human Value[10] in which child development specialists Nancy Curry and Carl Johnson discuss the research

NARRATIVE SENSIBILITY

Narrative pedagogy encourages free expression within appropriate boundaries.

on three different parenting/teaching styles—*authoritarian, permissive,* and *authoritative*—and how each style influences children's self-esteem.

Drawing from the work of Clarke-Stewart and Friedman,[11] Curry and Johnson explain that an *authoritarian* adult is "firm, punitive, unaffectionate, unsympathetic, detached, and sparing in their praise." *Permissive* adults "avoid[ed] laying down rules, asserting authority, or imposing restrictions. They tolerated their children's impulses—children were expected to regulate their own behavior and make decisions on their own." *Authoritative* adults were "firm, loving, and understanding—[they] set limits, but they also encourage independence." Curry and Johnson contended *authoritative* adults offered the best support for children's growth by showing acceptance, setting limits, and respecting their children.

In the situation with Chris and the boys, I was responding somewhere between the authoritative and the authoritarian style. I let them perform their skit in the private context of the studio, but I set limits concerning where they could perform it—an example of the authoritative. However, in being so abrupt and by not allowing any dialogue, I possibly bordered on responding in an authoritarian manner.

I came to see the importance of balancing the narrative (by seeking to understand through listening and open dialogue) with the normative in situations requiring boundaries. Just as I sometimes must reduce the normative if it carries too much weight on the mobile, sometimes I might have to limit the narrative. As Parker Palmer reminds me, "for a space to be a space, it must be open as well as bounded. Space without boundaries is not space, it is a chaotic void, and in such a place

---

10 Nancy E. Curry, and Carl N. Johnson, *Beyond Self-esteem: Developing a Genuine Sense of Human Value* (Washington, DC: National Association for the Education of Young Children, 1990).

11 Alison Clarke-Stewart, and Susan Friedman, *Child Development: Infancy through Adolescence* (New York: Wiley, 1987) 361-362.

no learning is likely to occur."[12] Enacting a narrative pedagogy did not mean giving unlimited space to the narrative. I must be open to dialogue, sensitive to context, trusting of my intuition, and accepting of the ambiguity, realizing that every situation calls for an "it depends" response.

Today I ask myself, "What if my ideas about what is appropriate subject matter does indeed change over time?" I still believe what Parker Palmer has stated, that children need clear boundaries for learning to take place. And I believe that being an authoritative adult and not a permissive or authoritarian one is better for the child, and, of course, dialogue is essential, not knee-jerk reactions. Today, however, I would not censor the skit. It was harmless. And it was highly creative! My response to

NARRATIVE SENSIBILITY

Self-understanding (especially of one's school culture and one's early sense of right and wrong) is critical in allowing children the freedom to transgress and develop their own aesthetic interests.

not allow it in the classroom for fear that the other students would start making all sorts of flatulent sounds was unfounded and untested. After reflecting on my beliefs, I see now that I was very much influenced by my ideas regarding school culture as well as how I had been raised.

12 Palmer, *The Courage to Teach*, 74.

CHAPTER 6

Art Classroom as Haven

"WELCOMING CHILDREN TO THE NEW WORLD OF KINDERGARTEN"

One of the most important gifts an adult can give a child is the gift of accepting that child's uniqueness.

FRED ROGERS

PEDAGOGICAL CONSIDERATIONS

One of my aims is to create a space where children feel secure, accepted, and free to take risks. I believe that children's emotions are the foundation for learning, and therefore I want children to have positive feelings about their art teacher, the art classroom, and their art experiences. Although this is my desire, I struggle to address all of the emotional concerns and diverse abilities within the wide age range of a K-1-2 classroom. The pressure to teach art in such a crowded space to children with such a wide range of abilities is an air current that keeps the mobile in constant motion. The moment I create a sense of balance, the emotional needs of the children tip everything off balance again.

The conversations about the following vignette began at the end of the school year when classroom teacher Alicia Jones and I had been concerned that a few of the older children in her K-1-2 classroom had formed cliques and left out the new kindergarteners. Wanting to avoid a similar situation the following school year, we decided to work together to form a more caring classroom community. To develop this idea, we proposed the idea of creating "a welcome book" for next year's new students, an idea that was enthusiastically received.

We began by having conversations in small groups, and we tape-recorded their responses to three questions. "What is your memory of the first day of kindergarten?" We hoped to talk about feelings—maybe this could be a place of identification, a place of empathy. We then asked, "What advice would you give to a new kindergarten student—especially if he or she missed their mom and dad?" We thought that ideas coming from their peers would speak to the new kindergarteners in their own language. And third, we asked, "What could we tell the new children about our school—what do you think they would like to know?" Again, we felt the voices of the children could speak to the new students in a way that said, "We've been there, and we understand." The children had also created drawings of the school, their classroom, and their teachers.

The following vignette depicts my reflections as I sat at home a week before the start of the new school year and began to assemble the "welcome book."

VIGNETTE—PREPARING "THE WELCOME BOOK"

I was in the process of reading the children's responses to the questions Alicia and I had posed to the previous year's students and was heartened by the positive memories shared by many of them. For example, Jack said, "I was shy at first, but when I met my teacher, I wasn't scared anymore." Becky said, "I remember meeting Rachel and playing house and doctor. I was feeling great that day!" As I continued to read, however, some comments gave me pause.

Campbell, a very bright child said, "I felt stupid all year long."

Mitchell, one of the most social boys in the class, shared, "I remember crying my eyes out, because I missed my mom and dad."

Shelley: I was mad at my mom and dad for sending me to kindergarten. I really missed my old preschool.

Jerry, a new second grader, who had come from a different school: On the first day I felt left out—like the bad kid.

Angie: I remember feeling nervous and really, really scared. I wanted to go home—because I was only four. And on top of that, it was the year that my dog died.

Although I knew that going to kindergarten was a major transition, the comments of children who had difficulty transitioning troubled me. As an art teacher, I usually do not see the children on their first day of school—or even their first week. Often by the time they come to art class, they are excited and feeling happy to be at school. Maybe adjusting to school is a greater task than I had imagined.

Reading their conversations and "listening" to the children who had difficulty with the transition reminded me of two previous situations. The first memory was about Jimmy, the second about Paula. Both were new kindergarteners.

Jimmy

Jimmy came to art class for the first time on his first day of school with the older children in a K-1 classroom. Based on the first graders' interest in stories and pets from last year, I decided to bring a pet kitten into the classroom for the children to meet. I shared with them a special book I had made about my cat, Cuddles Catnip Krakowski, who belonged to me when I was their age.

I asked all of the children to share stories about their pets and then invited them to create their own special books. The class had a number of children who loved to draw. I imagined the project to be a perfect fit.

All of the children, except Jimmy, spontaneously began to draw image after image in their books. At one point, I looked over at Jimmy's table and saw that he was crying. Busy with other children, I was relieved to see my work-study student walk over to see what was wrong. Checking with her at the end of class, I heard that Jimmy seemed to be afraid to put his ideas down on paper.

I remembered thinking, "Here was another child who was too hard on himself and felt that he had to be perfect before he drew. There was always one child who had difficulty adjusting to kindergarten." I also remembered feeling hopeless over the kindergarten-primary configuration that I had no control over. It did not occur to me that possibly I was part of the problem—that maybe I was not attuned to Jimmy's experience of my class and to his need to feel safe and competent. Maybe I had planned a lesson that did not connect with a new kindergartener's immediate concerns.

Paula

Paula was having trouble adjusting to school. Not only did she cry in art class, but she also cried all day in her other classes. She began to miss school, and I saw her only a couple of times during the first month. One day her mother phoned and said that Paula was afraid to come to art class. "You have to be kidding," I thought. "How could anyone be afraid of coming to my class?" I redirected the conversation back to Paula having difficulty adjusting to "all" of her classes. I discussed possible reasons why Paula might be having trouble with the separation (from mom!) and with transitioning to kindergarten.

After I hung up, I thought about what Paula's mother had said. I had a very challenging class that year. A number of first grade children behaved aggressively toward each other and constantly tested boundaries. I had to be very firm with them the first week—and many weeks after—to make sure that they understood my expectations and the classroom rules. If I did not address it now, I rationalized, it would only get worse. I could not deny that Paula was having difficulty adjusting to school in general, but in relation to art class, had I been too firm? Had I come across as scary—or even mean?

Both of these memories troubled me. I had always been committed to the emotional well-being of my students. How could I have been so insensitive? Why did I have trouble listening?

Returning to the preparation of the welcome book, I pondered my approach to the first day of school for my kindergarten students. Needing some company, I turned on the television, flipped through the channels, and saw that Mr. Rogers Neighborhood had just begun, and serendipitously, the theme of the week was "Mr. Rogers Goes to Kindergarten."

BALANCING SENSIBILITIES

Lacking in the preceding vignette is a sensibility that Maxine Greene referred to as "wide-awakeness."[1] I had been losing touch with the kindergarteners' experience of being in a multi-age classroom. In the situation with Jimmy, I had designed a lesson based on the first graders'

---

1   Maxine Greene, *Landscapes of Learning* (New York: Teachers College Press, 1978), 42.

interests from the previous year, assuming that the kindergarteners would have the same interests and concerns. In the situation with Paula, I responded to the older children who had difficulty with their impulses based on my previous experiences with them. In this K-1 configuration, my attention was more on the first graders than the kindergarteners.

With Jimmy and Paula, I seemed to rationalize away the children's feelings. "There's always one child." "If I don't go over the rules on the first day, their behavior will only get worse." "None of the other children are having difficulty, so the problem must be with the single child."

In Paula's case, I blamed the mother. In Jimmy's, I blamed Jimmy and the kindergarten-primary configuration over which I had no control. I thought, "Before the configuration changed, I never seemed to have any problems. It was always so easy to gear my lessons toward the kindergarteners' emotional interests." In both situations, I neither questioned my assumptions nor pondered what was important to the children. I didn't stop to rethink how the change in the classroom configuration might call for a change in my approach to the first day of school.

Five years earlier, when my school shifted to a K-1-2, all-in-one-class configuration, I had been very attuned to shifting the curriculum and rearranging my lessons to make sure that the kindergarteners were never left out. Further, I constantly questioned the rationale behind placing kindergarteners with older children and argued my position with both my colleagues and the administration. I was told that it was a trial placement, and if it did not work, the school would consider going back to a self-contained kindergarten.

When nothing changed after five years, I wondered if I were succumbing to apathy and passivity that Maxine Greene contends teachers can experience when they give in to educational practices over which they feel they have no control? She said that we might blame others—even those who were the victimized ones, instead of realizing that we could be pro-active in our own situations. "We stopped posing critical questions of our own." To become wide-awake, Greene said that we need to transcend our passivity— "to remain in touch with [our] original perceptions" and "to be present to oneself." We need to question our taken-for-granted assumptions and "break with the mundane."[2] Had my acquiescence to the system caused me to gradually lose touch with my original perceptions of the kindergarteners' concerns? Working on the welcome book re-awakened my awareness of the importance of listening more carefully to the children during their transition to school.

Watching Mr. Rogers Goes to Kindergarten, further awakened my need to re-focus on the kindergarteners' transition. According to Roderick Townley, Fred Rogers believed that transitions were one of the most important aspects of children's lives. Rogers said that we tend "to hurry through transitions and [try] to hurry our children through them as well. We might feel that these transitions were "nowhere at all" compared to what's gone before or what we anticipated next to come."[3] By focusing the theme for the week on the concerns of new kindergarteners, Rogers was acknowledging one of the major transitions in the lives of children.

Watching the show, I observed how Rogers created a safe and welcoming space between himself and his child audience. He communicated understanding for their concerns and validated the range of feelings that they might have about going to school. I was reminded that being a good teacher is more than knowing about children and about the subject matter. It is who we are in their presence. Mr. Rogers knew a lot about children and their development, but more than that, it was who he was—his way of being—that enabled him to touch their lives.

Mr. Rogers displayed what educator Max van Manen called sympathetic understanding:

> ...sympathy (literally, with-feelings) presumes not so much that we vicariously live in the other person but that the other person already lives in us, that we recognize the experience of the other person as a possible human experience—and thus as a possible experience of our own selves. But to open (our head

2   Greene, *Landscapes of Learning*, 2.
3   Roderick Townley, "Fred's Shoes: The Meaning of Transitions in *Mister Rogers' Neighborhood*," in *Mister Rogers' Neighborhood: Children, Television, and Fred Rogers*, eds. Mark Collins and Margaret M. Kimmel, (Pittsburgh, PA: University of Pittsburgh Press, 1996), 68.

and heart) to the inner life of the other we must orient ourselves to the other with care and love. Love is not blind but makes us see the other as other. So pedagogical sympathy attunes caringly to the inner life of the child, without confusing its own self in this inner life. In short, sympathy means pedagogically that the adult "understands" in a caring sense the situation of a child or young person.[4]

I wondered how Jimmy and Paula had experienced my presence in their lives. Had Jimmy found me at first to be indifferent and unavailable—too busy? Did Paula initially experience me as cold and uncaring? Did they find me to be sympathetic? Van Manen stated, "A teacher who is judged sympathetic by students tends to be described as warm, open, and understanding by them...This is a teacher who can pick up on the mood of the class, who can spot problems, to whom you can go if you have difficulties."[5] According to him, the opposite of sympathy is antipathy which is characterized by aloofness, coldness, indifference, unfriendliness. A teacher with this kind of orientation toward children is less likely to have a deep pedagogical influence on their lives.

I saw that Mr. Rogers was sympathetically attuned to the concerns of children. He was an example to me of how over the years he had listened closely to the narrative—the children, their interests, their feelings, their points of view—and how the narrative had informed everything he did and said on his television show. The narrative informed and shaped the normative—what he believed was important to address on his show.

Further, I saw that the concerns Mr. Rogers addressed were the same concerns that my K-1-2 students mentioned in their conversations for the welcome book. My students worried if they would like their teacher, if they would make friends, if they would be able to play, if they would cry, if they had snack, if they could make it to the bathroom on time. In his show, Mr. Rogers addressed each issue.

---

4   Max van Manen, *The Tact of Teaching: The Meaning of Pedagogical Thoughtfulness* (Albany, NY: State University of New York Press, 1991), 97-98.
5   van Manen, *The Tact of Teaching*, 98.

Remembering the words of the children and Mr. Rogers, and revisiting my prior understandings about first day worries, I carefully reconsidered my approach to the first day of school. Max van Manen contended that it was possible to be physically absent from children, but still have a sense of their presence in our lives—just as they could be right in front of you and be absent from your consciousness.[6] The children were now present in my consciousness.

As I began to prepare my lesson, I again confronted the challenge of not having met the children. I would have to rely on past understandings of children and my students' interests from previous years. My aim was to have a first day lesson where the kindergarten children would feel safe, relaxed, and welcomed. I also wanted the art experience to be pleasurable and engaging. What would best create this strong sense of well-being?

In the past, on the first day of class, I always introduced the new children to my classroom puppets—

NARRATIVE SENSIBILITY

Narrative pedagogy entails planning with heightened awareness, sympathetic understanding, and wide-awakeness.

The Talking Art Box and Felix, the Komodo dragon. The children loved these puppets and could not stop talking about them. Parents would come to my room asking to meet the Talking Art Box because they had heard so much about him. The children drew pictures for the puppets and constantly wrote notes to the Talking Art Box, dropping them into his mouth. The puppets helped to create an atmosphere that communicated, "This was a place where you can feel free to use your imaginations."

The presence of the Talking Art Box and Felix at the beginning and end of class had also become part of our classroom ritual. Curry stated, "Young children like and need ritual, to know what to expect, and in a sense to be in the know."[7] With this in mind, and after watching Mr. Rogers, I was reminded how he used puppets to help children deal with feelings such as parting, sharing, and growing up. I could use my

6   Max van Manen, *The Tone of Teaching*.
7   Nancy E. Curry, "The Reality of Make-believe," In *Mister Rogers' Neighborhood: Children, Television, and Fred Rogers*, eds. Mark Collins and Margaret M. Kimmel, 51-64 (Pittsburgh, PA: University of Pittsburgh Press, 1996).

puppets to help the children share their feelings about parting from parents, a former school, teachers, and routines, and entering a new school. Felix, the Komodo dragon, could feel sad because he missed his mom and dad. The children could offer him suggestions on what to do. I began to plan with heightened awareness of the children's emotional concerns a kindergarten lesson for the first day of school.

I decided that I would do an art project related to the theme of separation and transition. Of course, I would not use those words with the children. We would draw self-portraits and include in our drawing a picture of our favorite stuffed animal or toy. Over the years, I had seen these "transitional objects" present in the children's play and art. I remembered my niece, Julia, who even as a seven-year-old, still took her tattered stuffed bear to bed every night. Her bear appeared in many of her self-portraits in preschool. I remembered David, who would not draw for me for the first two months of school, and then one day, out of the blue, he drew a picture of "Puffy," his special pillow, and gently placed it inside the Talking Art Box. Yes—it was a significant theme that ran deep. Over the summer I had collected a variety of soft, velvety, textured fabric papers that resembled the fur, colors, and patterns of animals. We could use them for the stuffed animals in their drawings. The "soft and cuddly" materials gave a comforting feeling.

I always liked to begin the school year with an art project that was autobiographical in nature (such as self-portraits) so the children could experience from the beginning that their art is about themselves. Further, it helps to begin a dialogue about who they are and what they are interested in. It also helps to have a sense of their abilities in graphic representation without having to do a "formal assessment." Later their self-portraits become a bridge to talk about how artists make work about themselves and what interests them.

I decided to show the children a stuffed animal from my childhood, named Fluffy, a dog with long droopy ears, sad eyes, and a zipper on his back. At one time a music box behind the zipper played *How Much Is That Doggy in the Window.* In the past when I showed the children one of my beloved toys, I felt as if we made a closer connection. It seemed that they liked knowing that I had been a child like them.

I decided to prepare a wall space outside the classroom for their drawings. The children could dictate stories about their stuffed toys, and I would place their drawings next to their words, leaving me a visible trace of their thoughts. By displaying their drawings, the very next day, I hoped they would feel special and know that I valued their work. I wanted them to feel included in the school community. I wanted to encourage a dialogue between the child and his or her parent about the art—particularly on a theme connecting so closely to home.

During this week of preparing the classroom for the children's arrival, I organized the space to mirror the child's world. Hoping to invite the children to play with toys, I set out my collection of toys—dinosaurs, woodland animal, Star War action figures. I displayed artwork that I found appealed to children. I placed a print of Henri Matisse's *Goldfish* next to Scarlet, the classroom pet beta fish. I hung Patricia Renwick's *Stegovolkasaurus* art print next to a toy model of a stegosaurus, hoping to suggest interesting connections between the children and adult art. I also tucked some of my favorite stuffed animals into an art book corner. A teddy bear sat next to the book *Drawing Lessons from a Bear* and a shabby Curious George sat next to the book *Curious George Goes to the Museum.* I felt as if the stuffed toys would remind the children of some of their transitional objects and help them to feel more at home.

In the next chapter, I include a vignette illustrating how heightened awareness of children's emotional needs during the transition to kindergarten played out with one class.

CHAPTER 7

Art Classroom as Haven

CREATING SAFE SPACES

The classroom should be like an aquarium, mirroring
the cultures and interests of all who dwell in that space.

LORIS MALAGUZZI

PEDAGOGICAL CONSIDERATIONS

Because of the multi-age classroom configuration, only the kindergarten children come to school on the first day of class. On the second day, only first and second graders arrive. On the third day, all of the children come together. The reflections in the preceding chapter describe many of the issues I considered as I planned for the children's initial introduction to the art classroom. This vignette describes what actually unfolded.

VIGNETTE—THE FIRST DAY OF SCHOOL

The seven kindergarten children arrived at the art studio. They walked quietly, tiptoeing as if the floor were made of glass. They looked without touching and spoke in whispers. It was the kind of quietness that only a first visit could inspire. I found myself also speaking softly, mirroring their inquisitive and shy mood.

Ben broke the quietness. He asked excitedly, "You have a dinosaur in here?" He pointed to the stegosaurus on the ledge next to the Stegovolkasaurus art print. His question seemed to combine "Why was there a dinosaur in an art room?" and "How did you know that I liked dinosaurs?" Little did Ben know that I was thinking about children just like him when I placed the dinosaur on the entranceway ledge.

I acknowledged Ben's interest in dinosaurs and then welcomed the children to sit down at the table that I had prepared for them. I introduced myself and began sharing some ideas of what would be happening in our time together. Giving an overview, I believed, helped to give the children a sense of security. I then said that I wanted them to meet my art room friends.

> Immediately, pointing to the Talking Art Box, Ben asked, "What's that?"

> "That's my friend, the Talking Art Box. He lives in the art studio. Would you like to meet him?"

Immediately I sensed a shift in their mood and attention. They slipped easily into a world of fantasy; the Talking Art Box had cast his spell.

> "You see," I told them, "The Talking Art Box leaves me a message on a tape every morning for the children in my classes. When you come to class, I put this little tape recorder in his mouth and play it for you. Would you like to hear what he has to say?"

> They immediately nodded yes, still pondering whether a box could really talk. At their age, fantasy and reality were equally real.

I turned on the tape, and the Talking Art Box bellowed out in a voice that sounded like a friendly Wizard of Oz, "Hello, boys and girls. My name is the Talking Art Box. Welcome to the art studio. I've been waiting to see you. How are you today?"

The tape paused. The children entered into a dialogue and responded, "Good."

"I'm glad to hear it. I am, too," he bellowed. I hear that it is your first day of kindergarten. When I heard that you were coming today, I got very excited. Would you like to know a little bit about me?"

The tape paused again. "Yes," responded the children, their eyes riveted on his face.

"I'm a very special art box that lives in this art classroom. Inside me I have all sorts of fun things for us to do. Sometimes I bring my puppet friends. Sometimes I bring picture books. Sometimes I bring ideas for art projects. I have one of my puppet friends inside me right now. Would you like to meet him?"

The children replied, "Yes," and I walked over to the Talking Art Box to pull out Felix. Before I brought him out, the Talking Art Box finished his message. "Well, boys and girls, I am going to let your art teacher, Ms. Krakowski, get out my friend. I'll talk to you later. I'll sit right here so that I can watch you make art today. Bye, for now."

"Good-bye, Talking Art Box." "Good-bye." "Talk to you later." The children waved good-bye to their new friend.

I placed Felix on my hand and brought him out. He immediately buried his head on my shoulder, trying to hide from the children. "This is Felix. He's feeling a little shy today." Felix kept his head buried.

"Felix, I have some children that I'd like you to meet." Felix slowly turned his head around to take a peek and then immediately buried it again on my shoulder. His quick movements made the children laugh. "Felix, it's okay to feel shy. These children are new, too. This is their first day of school." He peeked again and then quickly hid his head. The children laughed again.

> Sean, one of the youngest boys, asked, curiously, "Why is he so shy?"

> Felix, who at this time only talked to me, whispered in my ear.

> "Felix says that he's a little sad because he misses his mom and dad." The children gave a compassionate look. They seemed to understand.

> I turned to Felix and said, "Felix, it's okay to feel a little sad." And then, I turned my attention to the children and said, as if I had this thought for the first time, "I know, maybe you could say something to make Felix feel better."

> Immediately they all had a suggestion. Marta, who seemed to be feeling very comfortable with school, said, "Tell him that's he's going to make lots of friends. You know, have some fun, make some friends, and then go home and be with his mom and dad."

> I turned to Felix, "Did you hear that, Felix? You're going to make lots of friends. Does that make you feel better?" Felix felt a little braver, looked at the children out of the corner of one pink eye, and nodded his head "yes."

> "You can tell him that he'll see his mom and dad at the end of the day. It's not as if they've gone away," said Amanda.

I turned again to Felix and said, "What do you think of that? Does that make you feel better?" Felix, beginning to become more energetic, again nodded "yes."

Ben took his turn in giving advice. "Tell Felix that his parents will be in his heart." Felix turned around and smiled at Ben, nodding his head up and down in agreement.

"He could draw a picture of his parents," said Eddie. Felix continued to respond affirmatively, growing less shy.

"You could bring in a special toy to play with," said Jason.

I took advantage of Jason's suggestion to move into the next part of our lesson, introducing my stuffed dog Fluffy. In return, the children told me stories about their stuffed animals. Just then Felix tapped me on the shoulder to remind me about our art project.

"Felix and I thought you might want to draw a picture of yourself with your favorite toy." The children welcomed the idea enthusiastically.

Because they had already shared stories about their favorite toys, I did not need to say much more. I showed them the materials, especially the special textured paper for their collage of their stuffed toy and gave every child a piece of white paper and a thin black marker. They began to draw themselves with the black marker and then used color. Many of them drew and cut out stuffed animals and glued them down; some drew their animal directly on the paper. As they worked, I wrote down their stories about their pictures. After we shared our stories with each other, it was time for the class to end.

"I think the Talking Art Box has a good-bye message for you," I said. I turned on the Talking Art Box, who once again bellowed out his message.

"I'm back, boys and girls. I had a wonderful time watching you draw today. I'd love to see your pictures." The tape paused. One by one the children held up their drawings for the Talking Art Box to see and told him what they had drawn. The tape resumed.

"Thanks for sharing your pictures with me. I'm looking forward to seeing you next week. You'll be in class with a lot of children that I know from last year. And Felix will be here, too. Good-bye for now. Have a great week."

"Good-bye, Talking Art Box." "Bye." "See you next week."

I turned off the Talking Art Box tape and put Felix back on my hand. He no longer hid his head on my shoulder and looked the children directly in their eyes.

"I think that Felix is pretty excited that he made new friends today. Look at how he is watching you. He's not feeling shy anymore."

Felix pretended to hide and made the children laugh again. And then I remembered something important.

"I forgot to mention this earlier. Do you see this little spot on the top of his head? It's darker than the rest of his skin, and it's very, very smooth. That's because Felix loves to be rubbed right in that spot. Kind of like the way your cat or dog loves to be petted under its chin or behind its ears. If you'd like, today when you leave, you can shake Felix's hand, or give him a hug, or rub him on his special spot."

It was time to go, and we said good-bye to one another. I stood by the door with Felix on my hand. One by one, the children left the art studio to go back to their homeroom. Already endeared to Felix, they gave him affectionate good-byes. Some gave him a hug. Some shook his hand. And every child rubbed his special spot.

BALANCING SENSIBILITIES

As I reflected on *The First Day of School*, I sensed that I had a different way of being with the children than in previous years. Responding to the children in a narrative frame of mind, I was present both to the children's mood *and* mine. I was also present to what William Ayers calls *childlikeness*.[1] By listening to the narrative, I created what the child development literature refers to as a *holding environment*.

Throughout *The First Day of School*, I was very attuned to the mood of the students and the classroom, what some researchers refer to as the *pedagogical atmosphere*.[2] As van Manen wrote, "Atmosphere is the way in which space is lived and experienced." It is also, he added, "the way that teachers are present to children and the way that children are present to

NARRATIVE SENSIBILITY

Narrative pedagogy entails:

♦ being present to the pedagogical atmosphere;

♦ discerning the children's emotions and mood, and

♦ being in touch with one's own childlikeness.

themselves and the teacher." "The sense of mood or atmosphere," he wrote, "is a profound part of our consciousness...Mood is a way of knowing and being in the world."[3] In my journal I wrote about the mood I sensed when in the presence of the children.

Throughout the class, I experienced a sense of peace. At the beginning of the lesson the children were noticeably quiet. I sensed their shyness. As the children became more comfortable with me—I sensed their becoming more relaxed—feeling more at home. When I introduced Felix, I sensed their tenderness and

---

1 William Ayers, *The Good Preschool Teacher* (New York: Teachers College Press, 1989).
2 See Bollnow, 1989; van Manen, 1986.
3 van Manen, *The Tone of Teaching*, 36, 32.

concern—they seemed to identify with him when he said that he missed his mom and dad.

At the end of class, I had a really good feeling—a wonderful warm, snuggly feeling—especially when they said goodbye to Felix and rubbed his special spot. I sensed that the children were happy. I sensed that they wanted to be there. I sensed that they wanted to come back again.

Throughout the lesson, I noticed that my sense of the mood guided my next response. Being present to the mood helped me to know—albeit intuitively—what to say to the children and how to proceed. As van Manen stated:

> To have a sympathetic capacity means that one is able to discern the subtle signs in a child's voice, glance, gesture, or demeanor. Sympathetically we sense what an experience is like for the child, or what mood the child is in—frustrated, stimulated, sad, bored, joyful, adventurous, fearful, gloomy, interested. In maintaining a sympathetic orientation to children, we are infected by the same mood, the same feeling, so that an even closer relation is formed between this child and ourselves.[4]

In contrast to the situation with Jimmy and Paula from the preceding chapter, remaining present to the children's mood in *The First Day of School* opened up more possibilities for the children to feel welcomed and secure. With Jimmy and Paula, I ignored their moods and adhered to my agenda. By doing so, I missed responding sympathetically. Jimmy, who was feeling insecure and afraid to draw, needed to feel safe. For Jimmy, emotional safety meant "being able to act, think, and feel without fear. It mean[t] being able to try an activity I'm not good

---

4   van Manen, *The Tact of Teaching*, 97.

at…It mean[t] being able to take risks and expose what I didn't know. It mean[t] being valued for who I was instead of how well I performed." [5]

Paula, who was feeling overwhelmed by a new school and unruly classmates, and an art teacher trying to control them, needed to feel welcomed and loved. For Paula, emotional safety meant, "seeing a smile on my teacher's face the first day of school instead of a list of rules that [was longer] than my arm."[6]

William Ayers said that teachers who are in touch with their *childlikeness* could connect with their feelings of childhood. "They have the capacity to see things as a child sees them." He gave the example of a preschool teacher, Anna, who responded to children out of her memories of being a child:

> When she holds a child, she remembers that sense of safety that comes with being in the strong arms of a friendly giant. When she comforts a crying child, she remembers the wonderful sense of relief and well-being that can follow sadness, sorrow, falling apart. She remembers feeling her mother's presence when she opened her lunch at school and saw the way the sandwich was cut. She knows how it feels to lie on a fluffy rug and kick your feet, to be caressed by the ribbon on the edge of a soft blanket…[7]

I sensed that I was in touch with my own childlikeness both as I planned the lesson and when I taught it with the children. In my journal, I wrote:

> *The moment I put Felix on my hand, something inside me lit up. I felt playful. I felt as if I was tapping into a deep reservoir of childhood playful memories. When I showed the children Fluffy, I remembered the comfort he brought me when I was a child. I remembered how it felt to hug him and how I took him to bed with me every night.*

5 Sugar in Bluestein, 2001, 8.
6 (Delisle in Bluestein, 2001, p. 8).
7 Ayers, *To Teach* (1989), 24.

Fred Rogers encouraged adults to stay connected to their childlike natures. In his own work, he frequently shared his childhood experiences with his viewers. When he visited the kindergarten classroom, he told the children that when he was their age, he liked to play with puzzles and with blocks. Edith Cobb[8] had studied the use of imagination in childhood and adulthood and arrived at the conclusion that adults who exhibited creativity drew from their memories of pretend play from childhood. Child psychologist Robert Coles reminded adults that they always needed to "struggle toward childhood and never forget or outlive it."[9]

As I continued to reflect on *The First Day of School*, I saw more clearly that listening to the narrative—the concerns of the children—and tailoring a lesson that acknowledged and validated their concerns helped to create a *holding environment*. The holding environment was a concept that has its origins in the child development literature.

The British child development theorist, Donald Winnicott suggested that early interactions between parent and child required a holding environment wherein the parent meets the child's needs. When the child's needs are met through "good-enough" parenting, they begin to develop a sense that the world is a friendly, fulfilling place and feel secure enough to move toward separation. [10]

Winnicott believed that within this relaxed state of the holding environment—what he also referred to as the *potential space*—the use of symbols developed.[11] One of the most significant early symbols is the *transitional object*. A transitional object is often a soft toy or a special blanket that has attributes of both parent and baby but is distinct from each. Winnicott viewed the creation of the transitional object as the baby's first true act of creativity, opening the door to the world of symbolic play. Within this potential space shared by parent and child, the child's symbolic play develops to include people and objects. In the safe, shared space, the child through play explores and navigates his or her inner world of the imagination and the external world of

---

8   Edith Cobb (1977)
9   Robert Coles. "Struggling toward Childhood. An Interview with Robert Coles," *Second Opinion* 18, no. 4 (1993), 71.
10   See also Curry,1996; Deri, 1978. Full citations in Bibliography.
11   Donald W. Winnicott, *Playing and Reality* (London: Tavistock Publications, 1971), 107-108.

reality. Winnicott believed the subject of this shared space widened to include artistic creativity and appreciation and eventually all cultural experience.

As I reflect on the notion that in the early years, creativity emerges in the shared space between child and adult, I realize how important it is for me to create a holding environment in the art classroom. By creating this shared space, I open the door and provide the building blocks for the children's present and future creative growth, arts learning, and appreciation. Art therapist Lani Gerity maintained that it was the task of art teachers or therapists "to create a *potential space*, an indestructible holding environment in the art room where the [child can] work safely, creatively, imaginatively, and constructively."[12]

Using puppets seemed to significantly support the creation of a holding environment. Gerity reported that in her art studio, "Puppet land" was one of the *potential spaces* where children and adults safely explored their inner feelings about their outer worlds. Fred Rogers used puppets on his television show to help children explore their feelings around

NARRATIVE SENSIBILITY

Creating a holding environment is crucial for narrative pedagogy.

themes that concern them. The children recognize themselves in his puppets, such as the fearful Daniel the Tiger or the shy Henrietta Pussycat. They also project feelings about their experiences onto the puppets. For example, King Friday could be perceived as an authority figure, and if the children were angry with their mother or father, they could express their anger at King Friday.

Rogers consciously created two worlds on his show—the real world of the Neighborhood and the imaginary world of the puppets in the Neighborhood of Make-Believe. He chose weekly themes that addressed an important issue such as growing up, the death of a pet, or going to kindergarten. Within the safe space he created, children could explore the theme in both worlds. When the children entered the Neighborhood of Make-Believe, the puppets helped them explore the theme at hand. For example, the week that Mr. Rogers invited the

---

12 Lani A. Gerity, *Creativity and the Dissociative Patient: Puppets, Narrative, and Art in the Treatment of Survivors of Childhood Trauma* (London: Jessica Kingsley Publishers, 1992), 76.

children to the kindergarten classroom, in the Neighborhood of Make-Believe, the puppets acted out a drama in which Daniel the Tiger was feeling scared because Lady Aberlaine told him he needed to know how to do addition and subtraction before he went to kindergarten. She was drilling him on math facts and telling him to "study, study, study." By the end of the week the issue was resolved, and Daniel learned that he did not have to know everything before he went to school. He discovered that school was a safe place where he would enjoy learning.

Entering the world of play and imagination allows children to navigate among their feelings about school more easily than if an adult explicitly tries to tell them, "Don't worry. Your teacher will be nice, and you will make lots of friends." Rogers believed that for the young child it was important to address the theme in both the real and play worlds.

In *The First Day of School*, through Felix, the Komodo dragon puppet, I created an inviting potential space for the children to enter the world of make-believe and share their advice, concerns, and feelings. Felix provided a safe, vicarious outlet for communicating their feelings. Felix had characteristics with which they could identify, such as shyness and a playful sense of humor. When the children offered Felix suggestions, in a sense they were giving suggestions to themselves. Through Felix, I provided a safe space for the children to negotiate the feelings of their inner world and the external reality of school.

The Talking Art Box also helped in their transition. When I turned it on to greet them, it captivated their attention, helping them to enter the realm of fantasy and feel more comfortable about being in the classroom. By saying good-bye at the end of class, Felix signaled a transition—it's time to return to your classroom. I believe young children, particularly on the first day of school, need time and support in preparing for what is to come next.

In the months that followed I saw a relationship develop between the children and both puppets. When the children arrived from a class where they had been engaged in more concrete learning such as reading or math, the Talking Art Box set the stage and tone for a shift in thinking. It was as if it was a transitional symbol saying, "Let's pretend."

Throughout the year Felix shared with them other concerns and interests. One week he talked about how much he loved to draw but did not want to show them a drawing of his self-portrait on the cover of his sketchbook because he felt as if he had to draw like the older children. When he showed them his drawing with wobbly lines that looked similar to some of their self-portraits, immediately they said, "Felix, that's good!" Their response gave him the confidence to show them the rest of the drawings in his sketchbook. He told them that sketchbooks were places where they could draw their favorite things. As he showed them his favorite things to draw—his mom, dad, the Talking Art Box, Ms. Krakowski, dinosaurs, robots—the children had fun guessing his subject matter and were on the edges of their seats to begin their sketchbooks. Together we talked about how everyone's drawing was special, and we did not have to compare it

NARRATIVE SENSIBILITY

Narrative pedagogy entails creating activities and rituals that mark transitions in the children's lives and in classroom/school events.

to someone else's or feel as if it had to be perfect. The freedom and motivation to create their self-portraits for their covers and to draw in their sketchbooks was markedly intense throughout the year.

If I had not listened closely to the children's memories of the first day of kindergarten, I would never have seen new possibilities for approaching the first day of school. Listening to the narrative and allowing the narrative to inform the curriculum helped me to create a potential space, a holding environment, where the children could create and feel comfortable making art.

The situations in the haven vignettes remind me that in order to balance the children's emotional concerns with my art lessons, it is essential to be present to their emotions. Greenspan stated that the children's emotions are the basis for all learning.[13] If I want children to be engaged in arts learning, then I need to be finely attuned to their feelings and understand their concerns.

The situation portrayed in The Welcome Book, reminds me of the importance of listening to individual children as well as the whole group. Karen Schultz stated, "Knowledge of the single child can be the basis for understanding and teaching a class." By listening to the particular child, teachers acquire "habits of mind"—ways of being, thinking, and

---

13 Stanley I. Greenspan, *The Growth of the Mind* (New York: Addison-Wesley, 1997).

acting that become a part of what she called a "listening stance." [14] In my situation, knowledge of a few children from Alicia's classroom, caused me to wonder if other children were experiencing difficulty in transitions. The situation awakened me to the need to rethink how I approached the first day of school with my new kindergarten classes.

My focus in planning the lesson was their emotional well-being. The emotional concerns of the children on the first day of art class in a sense became the curriculum. My perception of the narrative (e.g., some children might be having difficulty with transitions) guided my normative intentions. Jones and Reynolds remind early childhood educators of the importance of listening and considering children's emotions in what we make space for during the day. They wrote that "caregiving, expression of feeling, and resolving problems and interpersonal conflicts are not interruptions to the curriculum; they are the basic curriculum."[15]

Because all of the narrative and normative shapes exist in relationship to one another on the mobile, when any of the individual shapes are off balance, then the whole mobile can become out of balance. The emotions of a few can upset the balance of the whole mobile. I cannot ignore the emotions of even a few children.

Schultz referred to this notion of listening for balance within whole classroom conversations. Her ideas could also be applied to listening for balance within the emotional climate or mood of a classroom. She stated that balance was achieved by both listening and seeing. We can hear our students, but we can also visually read them.[16] Van Manen contended that teachers are constantly responding intuitively to the gestures, facial expressions, and tone of voices of their students and adjusting their pedagogical actions and responses accordingly. Being present to the pedagogical atmosphere and being in touch with the children's emotions, as well as my own, are important sensibilities for balancing the children's concerns, needs, joys, and fears with teaching an art lesson in the moment. Sensing how the children are feeling guides

---

14 Karen Schultz, *Listening: A Framework for Teaching across Differences* (New York: Teachers College Press, 2003), 36.

15 Elizabeth Jones and Gretchen Reynolds, *The Play's the Thing: Teachers' Roles in Children's Play* (New York: Teachers College Press, 1992), 90.

16 Schultz, 21.

me in knowing how and when to make adjustments; sometimes stepping back to give them more space; sometimes offering more scaffolding and direct instruction. Csikszentmihalyi suggested that to enter a state of flow, individuals need activities that are neither too challenging nor too simple. If I want children to derive aesthetic satisfaction from their work, then I need to be attuned to their capacities.

As much as it is possible for children to have aesthetic experiences, it is equally possible for them to have what Dewey called a "nonaesthetic experience":

> There is an element in all aesthetic perception. Yet when we are overwhelmed by passion, as in extreme rage, fear, jealousy, the experience is definitely non-esthetic.[17]

Art educator Deborah Smith-Shank studied elementary preservice teachers' early schooling experiences in art. Many of her students had vivid memories of being over-criticized by art teachers, shamed for lack of ability or even "left handedness," being excluded from art shows, receiving unfair grades despite one's best efforts, or experiencing art withheld as punishment.

NARRATIVE SENSIBILITY

By being attuned to children's emotional concerns and passions, a narrative pedagogy seeks to minimize non-aesthetic experiences.

Smith-Shank found that a number of pre-service teachers gave up on art and decided that it was not for them. She wrote, "...there [was] more than an element of passion in the memories of these experiences. The memories triggered extreme rage, fear, and jealousy, rendering art education definitely nonaesthetic for many of these preservice teachers."[18]

---

17 John Dewey, *Art as Experience* (New York: Putnam, 1934), 49.
18 Deborah L. Smith-Shank, "Mickey Mouse or Mapplethorpe: Metaphors for Understanding Art Anxiety," in *Preservice Art Education: Issues and Practice*, ed. Lynn Galbraith (Reston, VA: National Art Education Association, 1995), 37-38.

Because the art experience is imbued with such passion, being attuned to children's emotional concerns remains central in my teaching. When balancing the mobile, I need to be watchful of even the subtlest shifts between the narrative and normative and rely on my intuitive sensibilities to make adjustments at the slightest indication of disequilibrium. This was essential because if children are not experiencing a sense of well-being, then learning, development, and growth might be hindered.

CHAPTER 8

Art Classroom as Play Space

IMAGINING NEW POSSIBILITIES FOR CHILDREN

Play is often talked about as if it were a relief from serious learning. But for children, play is serious learning. Play is really the work of childhood.

FRED ROGERS

PEDAGOGICAL CONSIDERATIONS

One of my normative aims is for children to find meaning by engaging in art making drawn from their life experiences, which most often is play. One struggle in achieving this aim is creating time and space for what Brent Wilson referred to as "play art." Another struggle is creating time for me to observe the children's narrative interests so I can incorporate them into the normative curriculum. To resolve these struggles, I engage with children during scheduled and structured art classroom time and provide after-class and after-school time when the children can independently pursue self-initiated art making. The unstructured space of the after-class and after-school studio creates possibilities for more authentic art making, what some researchers refer to as "play art" as contrasted to "school art."[1] As Brent Wilson explains:

> This art has seldom been allowed into our highly controlled art classes. It is the spontaneous play art of young people...It has little of the polished lushness of classroom art, but once one learns to look at the tatty little drawings done in ball point pen on lined paper, a whole world of excitement unfolds. From play art we can learn why young children make art in the first place and why some keep on making it while others stop.[2]

Having extra time to pursue their play art affords opportunities for lingering, "being free from routines and fractions."[3] Lingering allows children to work according to their own rhythm rather than the pace set by the school clock. As the students linger over their projects, I am able to linger as well. I have time to listen to their stories, to gain ideas for new art projects, to relax into a narrative frame of mind.

While in a narrative frame of mind, I am able to pay close attention to the children's natural inclination to weave together play, story and art making. In the following vignette, I examine how my frustration with Max, an attention-seeking, first grader, clouded my vision and shut down my inclination to understand him, I share how letting Max's narrative about Godzilla into the art making space allowed me to reconnect with him and regain important narrative sensibilities.

Max showed little interest in making art, was easily distracted, and often appeared to be in his own private world. He would work on an art project for a few minutes, make a few quick marks, and then swiftly announce that he was done. Max had a habit of coming to talk to me every five to ten minutes. He loved animals, particularly reptiles, and

---

1   Arthur Efland (1976) writes about the school art style as extremely teacher-directed; it aims to please parents, and all of the art work in a display looks similar, with little individuality.
2   Brent Wilson, "The Superheroes of J. C. Holz: Plus an Outline of a Theory of Child Art," *Art Education* 27, no. 8 (1974): 3.
3   May, 1991, 144.

wanted to tell me everything about them. Felix, my Komodo dragon puppet, being a reptile, had captured his heart. Every day since our first art class, Max had stopped by the art studio to introduce me to one Felix's "relatives." One day, he had brought in his toy velociraptor from Jurassic Park to show me. The next day it was an allosaurus. I wondered who he would bring next. When Max dropped by, I felt he was talking *at* me, not *with* me. When I was unable to give him attention, he seemed to slip into his fantasy world. I wanted Max to have friends to work with and to engage in dialogues rather than monologues.

One hot Friday afternoon, Max's class arrived in the classroom. The room was stuffy; the children were tired and restless. It was their last class of the day—and the end of a very long third week of school. My agenda for the day was to invite the children to draw their self-portraits on the cover of their sketchbooks. I had introduced a similar activity the day before to another group of primary age students. I had shown them Felix's sketchbook, his self-portrait on the cover, and his drawings of his favorite people, places, and toys inside. They had loved it and drew enthusiastically throughout the whole class. Unlike yesterday, when the children could not wait to begin, Max's class could not concentrate for more than five minutes.

VIGNETTE—FELIX MEETS GODZILLA

Max was unusually restless. He walked up to me—the fifth time since the beginning of class—tugged on my shirt, and asked, "I have a new relative that I want Felix to meet. Can I go get him out of my locker?"

"Who is he?" I responded.

"I can't really tell you. It's a secret."

"No. I'd like you to finish your self-portrait first. We could have him visit another time," I responded, knowing that I had 23 other children to attend to as well. Max already was having a hard time focusing on

his sketchbook cover. I thought he did not need one
more distraction.

Max returned to his sketchbook and began to draw his self-portrait.
Without looking in the mirror, he worked in a rhythm, creating patterns
of teeth and ears all over his face. I could see that he was amused by the
final result. Two minutes later he was done.

He then opened his sketchbook and drew a portrait of what was
really on his mind. I thought it was a drawing of Felix until he wrote
the word, "GODZOLA" on top of his drawing.

> "Can I show my picture to Felix?" he asked. Without
> waiting for my response, Max walked to the front of
> the room where Felix was resting on his puppet stand.
> "Well, Felix, what do you think?" To get a reply, he
> nodded Felix's head up and down to say "yes."

Max continued to play with Felix instead of drawing in his
sketchbook. I sighed. Before long, he was by my side, tugging on my
shirt, asking again if he could bring a relative down from his locker to
meet Felix.

> Giving in, I asked, "So who do you have in your
> locker?"
>
> He whispered in my ear, "Godzilla."
>
> "Oh, really?" I responded with some curiosity.
>
> Capitalizing on my interest, he asked, "Can I get him?"
>
> I hesitated once again, not wanting to lose control
> of my already restless class. But I took a risk. "Sure.
> Why not?" Max's face lit up, and he ran upstairs to his
> locker.

In a matter of seconds, Max returned with a 15" plastic toy model
of a horrible-looking beast. "I'd like you to meet Godzilla," he said,
expecting me to shake its slimy, scaly hand. I shook its hand. The
expression on its face and its pose looked quite violent.

Attached to Godzilla was a long cord and a remote-control switch shaped like a green army tank. The tank looked like it was about to shoot bullets. Max pressed the tank button. Godzilla opened its mouth with a look of horror and then froze still, as if warding off the tank attack.

Godzilla immediately attracted the attention of the rest of the class—in particular, two of the kindergarten boys, Joey and Eric. They joined Max in pressing the remote button to make Godzilla roar and freeze. I thought to myself, "What was the attraction of this creature —who was obviously a hundred times more interesting than drawing a self-portrait on the cover of one's sketchbook?"

Sensing that this was a possible significant moment and curious to see what might happen, I invited Max and the two other boys to stay after class. As we sat together at one of the art tables, I learned that Godzilla was not the horrible beast I thought it was—in fact, it was quite the opposite. "His name is Tiger," Max informed me. "And he's very gentle. He's also an orphan."

Max would have been content to spend the whole time detailing Godzilla's life without ever using the art materials themselves—unlike Joey and Eric who were intently drawing pictures of their favorite Godzilla movies. But I wanted to engage Max, too. So, when he took Godzilla to meet Felix, I asked, "Would you like to make a drawing for Godzilla—I mean, Tiger? He may enjoy watching you the way Felix watches you draw."

Max eagerly opened his sketchbook and picked up a marker. "I have the exact perfect house for him," he said as he began to draw a house that looked part X-ray and part blueprint. Here's a porch and this is a bone hanging on a string."

I imagined that the bone was Godzilla's dinner.

"Here's another bone, and now I'll draw a mirror. He can look in the mirror and see how much he's grown. Now this will be the bedroom. I'm going to draw him a soft, comfy bed." I had begun to see that Max had a strong identification with Godzilla and was projecting feelings about himself (and how much he had grown) onto the creature.

I was struck by how he nurtured Godzilla. I had never seen Max so deeply engaged. Max then turned to Felix to show him his drawing.

"Okay, Felix, you be the judge. What do you think?" He put the puppet on his hand and nodded his head up and down.

"Thank you, Felix," said Max. And then he turned to me and exclaimed, "Felix thinks it's great."

I smiled and agreed. Perhaps Godzilla meeting Felix was the connection that I had been searching for.

When it was time to go, I asked Max and the boys if they would be interested in coming in again. They could use other materials, such as clay and wood, and make things for Godzilla.

"Clay!" Max said, "That gives me an idea. I could make a cave for Tiger. I could make a cave out of rocks, a door that would have to be really, really big. And a bed. Don't forget we have to make him a soft, comfy bed. With covers. We can't forget the covers."

Although I wanted to hear more of his ideas, the boys had a schedule to follow. It was time for them to return to their homeroom and then get on the bus that would take them home.

Max gathered up Godzilla and put Felix back on his stand. He whispered something fondly in Felix's ear and pretended to have Felix shake Godzilla's hand. He then turned and asked if he could come in next week and work on Godzilla's house. I said that I would love to have him come in. Within a few seconds, he was out the door and off to his homeroom.

I watched him leave, amazed by what had transpired. For the first time, Max had worked on an art project for more than a few minutes or shown an interest in coming to the after-school art studio. In the following weeks and months Max came into the art studio during free periods. With each visit he brought a new toy reptile to star in his next art project. He drew on page after page in his sketchbook. He always took Felix off his puppet stand to join us. Felix had to give Max his final approval, which was always "yes."

Within a few weeks Max began to tell me about art projects that he was working on at home and school. He and a younger student in his homeroom began to draw and invent treacherous mazes together. I was pleased that his art interests and friendships were growing. I also sensed a change in our relationship. I could not yet get specific, but I began to see Max in a new light. I no longer felt drained when I was around him. Nor did I feel as impatient when he talked nonstop. I actually began enjoying the time that we shared together. Sensibilities of a narrative frame of mind reasserted themselves.

BALANCING SENSIBILITIES

Reflecting on what kept me from initially connecting with Max, I referred to my journal. I had drawn two sketches to help me visualize and understand what had transpired between Max and me. The first sketch, "Worlds Apart," depicted the distance between my normative world and Max's world of fantasy. In my sketch, Max and I did not share a common space.

Figure 1

Around the drawing of myself, I captured my fleeting thoughts in cartoon bubbles: "Max never seems engaged." "Max is a spacey little boy." "Max is not entering in. Maybe I should just ignore him." "Why can't Max be like the other children?" "I hope he doesn't try to talk my ear off." "It's hopeless. I give up." Although in the past I tried to connect with Max, the drawing showed that I had given up. In pondering how I now saw Max, I was reminded of William Ayers provocative questions:

> When teachers look out over their classrooms, what do they see? Do they see the students, or do they see "a collection of deficits, or IQs, or averages? Who are the students? What dreams do they bring? What experiences have they had, and where do they want to go? What interests or concerns them, how have they been hurt, what are they frightened of, what will they fight for, and what and whom do they care about?"[4]

I returned to my journal to see what image I held of Max:

> *Max is very gentle and caring, especially toward animals. However, he is very clingy. When he talks to me, it is nonstop. It's as if I do not matter, except to be there to listen to him. He seems anxious. He is constantly at my heels, barraging me with facts about his toys and other inanimate objects. It's really odd. I feel totally drained when I am with him for more than a few minutes. I feel as if the life is sucked out of me. Sometimes I find myself wanting to avoid him when I see him coming. If he could, he would monopolize all of my attention. I feel that I need to be giving my attention to all of my students, not just one.*

Although I saw Max's gentle and caring side, I also saw him as clingy, needy, annoying, exhausting, and draining. That was the image that I had begun to carry around in my mind, an image I found unsettling as I thought about the philosophy of Reggio Emilia schools:

> Each of us has his or her "image of the child," which is reflected in the expectation that we have when we look at a child...Some focus on what children are,

4   Ayers, *To Teach*, 25, 28.

what they have, and what they can do, while others, unfortunately, focus on what children are not, do not have, and what they are not able to do. The teachers in the preschools of Reggio Emilia carry an image of the child as "active, competent, and strong, exploring and finding meaning—not as predetermined, fragile, needy, and incapable."[5]

During Max's kindergarten year, my mission, so to speak, was to figure out how to connect to him. I was treating Max more like an object for analysis than a real child. On the most draining days, I wondered if I truly liked him. Max was part of the most challenging kindergarten-primary class that I had ever taught. At least half of the children in my estimation had some kind of learning disability or emotional difficulty. I told a colleague one day, "At the end of art class, I feel as if the life has been sucked out of me. The children are so needy. Every few seconds someone comes up to me, asks for help, and wants my undivided attention. Also, they always seem to be picking on each other. I feel so wasted after they leave."

My colleague jokingly responded, "I have an art teacher friend who calls these children life-suckers."

"Life-suckers!" I laughed, feeling a twinge of guilt that I would ever use such a label with a child.

Focusing on the children's deficits prevented me from seeing who they were. As Ayers writes, "taking notes on children's deficiencies does not tell you about the children. It does not tell you what they care about or how they learn. It doesn't offer you any insights or clues into how you might engage [them] in a journey of learning, or how you might invite [them] into the classroom as a student."[6]

Classifying was my way of getting a handle on understanding Max. He was definitely different. At times I talked about Max as "a funny

---

5   Carlina Rinaldi, "Reggio Emilia: "The Image of the Child and the Child's Environment as a Fundamental Principle," in *Bambini: The Italian Approach to Infant/Toddler Care*, eds. Lella Gandini and Carolyn P. Edwards (New York: Teachers College Press, 2001), 50, 51.
6   Ayers, 30-31.

kid" or suggested that he might have a mild form of autism. In an essay titled Pedagogy is Child-Watching, van Manen cautioned:

> Once I call a child "a behavior problem" or a "low achiever," or once I refer to him or her as someone who has a specific learning style, a particular mode of cognitive functioning, then I am inclined immediately to reach into my portfolio of instructional tricks for a specific instructional intervention. What happens then is that I forego the possibility of truly listening to and seeing the specific child.[7]

Imprisoning children with categorical language, van Manen believes, is a form of "spiritual abandonment."

Returning to the sketches in my journal, I searched for the point at which my normative world and Max's fantasy world came together. When Max whispered that he had Godzilla in his locker, he sparked my curiosity, perhaps tapping into my own childhood fascination with monsters. My curiosity prompted the invitation for Max and the two boys to stay after class, giving me a chance to truly listen as they shared their stories about Godzilla.

NARRATIVE SENSIBILITY

Seeing the child's abilities (rather than deficits) and having an 'image of the child' as strong and competent helps to maintain a balance between the normative and the narrative.

Rinaldi writes that listening begins with emotion— "behind the act of listening there is often curiosity, a desire, a doubt, an interest."[8] As early childhood educator Vivian Paley writes, "The key is curiosity." When we demonstrate wondering, questioning, and curiosity about what children do and say, they feel respected. The child thinks, 'What are these ideas I have that are so interesting to the teacher? I must be somebody with good ideas.'[9]

When I became curious and said, "yes," my frame of mind changed from the normative to the narrative. As I loosened my control and my

---

7   van Manen, The Tone of Teaching (1986), 18.
8   Rinaldi (2001a), 80.
9   Paley, "On Listening to What Children Say," 122.

agenda, I began to open to possibilities for my relationship with Max. A second image I had drawn and titled, "Shared Space," shows Max and me sitting together at the art table with me smiling as Max worked on an art project with Felix, Godzilla, and some of Felix's "relatives" nearby. Rather than focusing on Max's weaknesses, I had begun to appreciate his imagination, curiosity, sensitivity, and playfulness. In our shared space, I began to see possibilities for him to engage in meaningful art making—both in my classroom and on his own. I had found what Csikszentmihalyi and Hermanson call "a hook," an intrinsically intriguing interest that can motivate the child's desire to make art.

Finding a hook is a necessary first step, but for meaningful art making to continue, Csikszentmihalyi and Hermanson indicate that teachers must engage children and sustain their

> **NARRATIVE SENSIBILITY**
>
> Genuine curiosity about the child's interests and fantasies forestalls categorization and allows for connections between normative and narrative pedagogical elements.

interests by forming strong and clear "soulful connections." Art making that draws upon the children's senses, feelings, and imagination, not merely their thoughts, skills, and information, has the potential to nourish the child's soul. By providing a variety of sensory and tactile materials, a safe environment, and my interested presence, Max became absorbed with his personal, deeply satisfying reptile themes.

When art making becomes absorbing and intrinsically rewarding, Csikszentmihalyi and Hermanson state that the conditions for flow—a state of optimal pleasure—are present. As the children experience the pleasure of flow, they are motivated to continue to create. Their skills increase, and they become more confident in their abilities. When the teacher offers children choices and the freedom to express themselves without fear of judgment, they are able to remain in a state of flow. Max's desire to pursue art projects outside of class on his own and with his friends indicated he was beginning to find art making pleasurable.

"Shared Space"

Figure 2

By including Max's toys in the "Shared Space" drawing, I illustrated Susan Deri's concept of a good "play space," in which children play alone within the security of the caring adult's presence. In this quiet play space, the adult can offer usable objects for play, and children, free of parental pressure, can choose what they need. Creative playing arises from this shared, relaxed state. Deri also wrote that the caring adult's responsive, affirming eyes and face function as a mirror, "reflecting the loved image of the child to the child." "The child internalizes the message that they exist in the world and their existence is good and enjoyed by the [caring adult]." [10]

10 Susan Deri, "Transitional Phenomena: Vicissitudes of Symbolization and Creativity," in *Between Reality and Fantasy*, eds. Simon Grolnick and Leonard Barkin (Northvale, NJ: Jason Aronson, 1978), 55-57.

Within our shared space, I functioned *in loco parentis*, creating a space where Max could freely explore his creative and artistic interests in the presence of a caring adult. I provided the art materials and let him freely choose what he wanted. Max became calm

NARRATIVE SENSIBILITY

Creating a quiet, shared "play space" offers opportunities for children to explore freely and internalize their worth as individuals in the world.

when we were together, and he had my undivided attention. Our shared space seemed to create a sense of emotional safety, a kind of holding environment.

Early childhood art educator Charles Bleiker wrote that when children draw, they often identify with certain themes or with a character, animal, or object that has deep significance for them. For example, a child who repeatedly draws airplanes might be fascinated with the "freedom, power, elegance, or complexity of airplanes and might wish to possess these qualities." Bleiker shared the story of a young girl who from age three drew cats and lions, which he suggested, represented her "growing awareness of her own power and strength." In one telling drawing, [the child] drew a menacing cat chasing a frightened dog under the heading of "Pussy Power."[11]

Perhaps Max's fascination with Godzilla (and Tiger, his gentle alter ego) was a projection of his feelings of power as well as conflicted feelings over anger and aggression. I am not suggesting that art teachers can or should offer psychoanalytic insights into their students. I am, however, suggesting (as did child development expert Nancy Curry) the importance of creating shared spaces where children can move comfortably between their subjective world of play and feelings and their objective, external world.

Not only did our shared space provide Max with opportunities to combine play and art making, but it also provided possibilities for me to have a more caring and compassionate relationship with Max. In his classic text, *I and Thou*,[12] the existential philosopher Martin Buber introduced two possible relationships between humans: I-Thou and I-It. In an I-Thou relationship, we are open to the presence of another human

---

11 Bleiker, 51-52.
12 Martin Buber, *I and Thou* (New York: Charles Scribner's Sons, 1970).

being, and we see that person as whole and unique. Buber advocated that teachers need to be concerned with the child as a whole, "both in the actuality in which [s/he] lives before you now and in his [or her] possibilities, what [s/he] will become."[13]

Initially when Max came to kindergarten, I related to him as a unique individual and listened intently. As time progressed and I became drained by his clinginess and need for attention, I withdrew, my listening waned, and my relationship with Max disintegrated into an I-It relationship. My stance became one of "an observer" of Max as I began to focus narrowly on his external traits and to ignore what was within him.

The shared space of imaginative play and art making allowed me to reclaim my earlier interest in Max, not as an object of curiosity, but as a real, multi-dimensional human being. Shifting to a stance of "perceiver," let me appreciate his idiosyncrasies and his unique way of being in the world. I began to genuinely like him. In our shared space, the possibility of an I-Thou relationship opened up.[14]

"Letting the child happen to me"[15] creates an openness within me; an openness to be changed; an openness to become aware; an openness to listening with my whole being. As Flickinger writes:

> ...hearing and listening are never purely sensory acts. We may hear the same sounds, but we listen for the meaning that the sounds evoke. And so, what is heard depends on who is listening...How we listen depends on the relationship we have with the one to whom we are listening.[16]

Similar to listening, van Manen writes, "How and what we see in a child is dependent on our relationship with the child." A teacher

---

13 Martin Buber, *Between Man and Man* (New York: Macmillan, 1965), 104.

14 In *Between Man and Man*, Buber contrasts three stances. An "observer" is primarily intent on noting and writing up the child's traits. An "onlooker" sees what the child presents but makes no effort to remember. A "perceiver" is one who is becoming aware and experiences that child as a whole.

15 John Stewart, "Forward," in *The Reach of Dialogue: Confirmation, Voices, and Community*, eds. Rob Anderson, Rob Cissna, and Kenneth N. Arnett (Cresskill, New Jersey: Hampton Press, Inc., 1994), viii-xx.

16 Aprile Flickenger, "Therapeutic listening." *Phenomenology + Pedagogy* 10 (1992): 186.

must not observe a child as "a passerby"—or *onlooker*—but must keep "in view the total existence of the developing child."[17] Over time as my relationship with Max grew, I began to see him as a child who was lovable, humorous, compassionate, creative, unique, and gifted. As William Ayers reminds me, I must "avoid blindness" and recognize that there was always more to know. "Staying open to mystery…is to allow students their full humanity."[18]

NARRATIVE SENSIBILITY

I-Thou relationships allow me to perceive children with their full humanity and remain open to mystery. In this shared space of listening and seeing, possibilities for growth—my own and the children's—can flourish.

---

17 van Manen, *The Tone of Teaching*, 16, 18.
18 Ayers, *To Teach*, 49.

CHAPTER 9

Art Classroom as Play Space

WAYS OF WORLDMAKING

*Place is crucial and it shapes and constrains the stories
that are told or, indeed, that could be told.*

JEROME BRUNER

PEDAGOGICAL CONSIDERATIONS

Three years before the situation in this vignette took place, I had begun to invite children into the art classroom during unscheduled after-school time so they could have more opportunities for unstructured art making, a place to play with the art that they made, and a space where I would have more time to able to listen, observe, and interact with them in smaller groups. On some days, I would sit down and be a part of their self-directed activity, and on other days I would listen to their conversations while cleaning up or preparing for the next day's lessons.

School had been in session for a few months. We had done a number of beginning-of-the-year autobiographical art activities, and now, as I was cleaning the classroom, I was listening for possible directions for more in-depth, extended projects.

I did not plan the events depicted in the following vignette. Rather, with heightened awareness I was attuned to the children's self-initiated learning. Reciprocity can happen when children become guides to the teacher's learning. Such was the case in this vignette.

Loris Malaguzzi wrote that we have within ourselves an image of the child that directs us as we relate to a child. This image—guided by our beliefs and theories about children— "pushes us to behave in certain ways"; it orients us as we talk, listen, and observe the child.[1]

The learning space we create for the children is guided by the image we hold of them. My response to children is guided by my image of them as "symbol weavers,"[2] who weave together the symbol systems of play, story, and art making to communicate meaning. The symbol-weaving natural inclination of young children often results in what I refer to in this chapter as Worldmaking. In Worldmaking, children create a small world inhabited with one or more characters. They create all kinds of accessories for the characters or for the world itself. The children then play with their characters and tell stories. Worldmaking can be two-dimensional as in drawing a tree home for a squirrel family or three-dimensional as in creating a clay home for a squirrel family.

VIGNETTE—MINIATURE WORLDS

It began with a squirrel sitting on the trash dumpster outside the art classroom window. Isabel, Rachel, and Josh had come in during after school hours to work on their wire and glass bead sculptures of autumn leaves. All of a sudden Isabel said, "Look, there's a squirrel outside our window!"

Immediately and without hesitation Rachel announced, "I'm going to draw that squirrel." She confidently walked over to where the paper and black felt tip pens were stored, picked out her materials, and returned to her seat facing the open window and the squirrel.

---

1   Loris Malaguzzi, "Your Image of the Child: Where Teaching Begins," *Child Care Information Exchange, 96* (1994), 52.
2   See Anne H. Dyson, 1989, 1990.

Isabel chimed in, "I want to draw one, too." Within seconds, Josh followed their lead.

"I really have a good idea," Rachel declared. "I'll need two pieces of paper to make a pretend squirrel home. It's like a people's house. Did you ever hear the story, *In a People's House?* It's from Dr. Seuss, and it's like this." She began to chant, "In a people's house you see chairs; you see bears; in a people's house. In a people's house, you see toothbrushes; you see walls; you can find all kinds of things in a people's house."

Responding to Rachel's idea, Isabel, and Josh both began to draw homes for the squirrel.

"I'm making a tree house," announced Isabel.

"I'm making a palace," added Josh, taping two pieces of paper together the way Rachel had done.

Sensing the importance of this moment, I sat down next to them to listen and observe. I basked in the relaxed atmosphere of not having the pressure to attend to 24 children at one time.

The children were relaxed too. Every fifteen minutes or so Josh would burst out in a song that he improvised on the spot for his newly created "Squirrel Opera." The children would occasionally crawl under the table and pretend they were squirrels and then return to their seats to draw.

As they continued with their drawings, I observed how fluidly they changed their ideas in midstream and how easily they influenced each other. Rachel who had begun by drawing a "people's" house for her squirrel changed her idea to a tree house after seeing Isabel's. Josh decided to turn his palace into a squirrel resort with lodges. He later changed it into a squirrel hotel when Isabel announced that her house had a million squirrels in it— "like in a hotel."

Isabel's older third grade sister, Greta, entered the art classroom, and seeing their drawings, asked, "Can I watch?" Together all of the children responded, "Do you want to make a home?" Immediately joining in, Greta began to draw an outside view of a tree. Picking up another piece of paper, she began to draw the inside of her tree, dividing its interior into five large rooms.

As the children drew, they narrated their ideas. Josh announced, "I'm drawing all these knobs on the doors. You have to pick the right one. If you pick the wrong one, it's a really bad smell!"

Rachel shared, "My house is going to have many rooms and a swimming pool." She then drew a row of three trees, connecting them with secret passageways, adding more rooms as well as the swimming pool. She looked at how far her drawing had progressed. Aware that she had initiated the idea of drawing the squirrel's home, she declared, "It's all because of that one little squirrel!"

Josh began to think of a name for his squirrel. "I think I'll call him Mr. Squirrel."

Rachel then said, "I'm writing at the top of my drawing—A Squirrel's Life." She spelled it—A SQOLR'S LIFE.

Josh interrupted, changing his mind about his squirrel's name. "He's Mr. Nut. That's what I'll call him."

Rachel, looking at Isabel's tree house, said, "Your tree looks like a weeping willow. Mine's just an ordinary squirrel with a huge house." She began to chant the Dr. Seuss rhyme again, "There are bedrooms; there are tables; there are beds; there are walls in a squirrel's house."

Isabel, returning to her drawing, told the group, "My squirrels are going to go disco dancing." She drew a disco ball from the ceiling of one of her rooms. She drew a black dress on her squirrel with its tail sticking out the back. "I'll make her dancing." Watching Isabel, Rachel drew a disco ball, too.

Greta, who had not shared anything yet, began to describe her picture. "My squirrels are naked except for the babies." Pointing to the rooms, she explained, "The dad's a carpenter. He's going to make the girls' and boys' bedrooms the exact same shape." Greta's dad was also a carpenter. Pointing to her baby squirrels, she said, "This one is called Pooh, and this one is called Acorn. They're the children. Here's their bedroom. I'm making them have huge tails so they can balance. I put acorn mush inside the pillow. The squirrels eat their blankets and pillows because they are made of acorn mush. Now I'm drawing acorn chocolate chip cookies." As she drew, Greta began to narrate the history of her squirrels. "In the olden squirrel days, they used acorn mush. One squirrel, who they called the god, said they should make acorn mush."

Rachel then announced, "In my squirrel home, it's close to Hanukkah. I'm going to make a menorah."

Isabel then shared, "This room is for if anybody drowns." A theme of safety began to appear.

Josh jumped in, announcing, "I'm making a jail," foreshadowing the arrival of bad guys. Isabel thought the jail was good idea in case anyone stole anything. Then she said, "Hey, I'm going to make a parachute. My squirrel needs a parachute." She drew two squirrels flying in a parachute in the sky above her tree house. Rachel decided to make one, too.

Rachel then announced her newly inspired idea. "Mine's going to sit in a hot tub." She writes the words "HAT TAP" above a tub of hot water.

Isabel interrupts with another idea, "Hey, I'm making a playground." At this point, her drawing had begun to be quite full (see Figure 3).

Figure 3: Isabel's Squirrel Home

Rachel, returning to the hot tub, said, "Another reason you can tell it's a hot tub is because there are bubbles coming up." She drew the bubbles and a squirrel standing in a bikini on the edge of a tub. As she proudly looked at her drawing, again she announced, "It's all because of that one squirrel!" She had the same sense of wonder as she did when she said it the first time.

Throughout their conversation, I continued to listen and observe. I wanted to have a sense of where to go next with their ideas, and so we talked about possibilities. I learned that they wanted to transform their drawings of their squirrel homes into clay. Greta especially wanted to make clay bedrooms and weave little blankets for her squirrel beds. Isabel and Josh wanted to write books about their squirrels.

As I talked with the children, their imagination sparked mine. Maybe they could turn their drawings into three-dimensional paper sculpture tree houses where they could construct the interior and exteriors. Maybe they could make miniature squirrel families and backyard animal friends out of oil-based clay to live in their homes and to visit each other. I also remembered past projects at the school for blind children where students made underground homes out of clay for little toy animals. They had enjoyed working on them for days. Underground homes for burrowing animals could be another possibility.

As our time together ended, Rachel not wanting to stop, asked, "Can we do this tomorrow?" I welcomed her interest and said that they could.

After they left, I located all of my art prints, miniature toy woodland animals, and picture books of backyard animals that live in real and imaginary homes. I called the natural history museum loan collection and discovered that I could borrow squirrels, chipmunks, mice, rabbits, and birds. I decided to borrow the squirrels first. I then sketched and mapped out all of the connections I could think of. Their initial ideas held possibilities for both real and imaginary animal worlds. I sensed that the children's interest would appeal to their whole class.

The next day Rachel and Isabel came in to finish their drawings. When they were done, I invited them to collaborate on a three-dimensional home in clay for the miniature toy squirrels. After an intense discussion over whether their home would be realistic or have human features, they reached a compromise and chose to make an imaginary home the first day and a real one the next. As they worked in clay, a drama about two squirrels, Fuzzy Wuzzy and Nutty, emerged. As they played, new ideas of what to make in clay evolved. Their play and art making became one.

"Hey, I have an idea!" announced Isabel. "Let's have them go on a sleepover. I'll make bunk beds." She molded a piece of clay into the shape of a bed.

"I think we should have food for them also. I'm going to make acorn pizza," added Rachel, flattening a ball of clay to make a circle for the crust.

As I observed the girls working for the next two hours, I had a clearer sense of where to begin with their whole class. I imagined going outside with them to look for signs of animals preparing for winter, and then returning indoors to model clay homes for our miniature toy backyard animals. It was growing colder outside, and our animals would need a safe home to protect them from the cold weather and predators. After they modeled their homes in clay, we could go on a nature walk to search for natural materials to "accessorize" their clay homes. Seeing how their interests unfolded, possibly we could then explore the idea of creating three-dimensional tree homes for miniature clay squirrels.

In the weeks and months that followed, Rachel and Isabel's class became deeply immersed in an exploration of the real and imagined lives of backyard animals, especially squirrels. Their class inspired the other primary classes to pursue this interest. The theme turned out to be a fertile one and carried us through winter—when our animals hibernated—and into spring—when they began to have babies. I found myself in a game of catch, tossing back and forth ideas between the children and myself.

Although I knew that their interest in the squirrel was a significant one, little did I know at the time that Rachel's impulse to draw its home would awaken such a rich yearlong exploration of nature, play, and Worldmaking. Rachel was right. "It all began with that one squirrel."

BALANCING SENSIBILITIES

In *Miniature Worlds* I sensed the significance of the children's interest in squirrels, not only for these four children, but for their whole class as well. Because I had been searching for where to go next with the curriculum, I was open to hearing their ideas. Inhabiting the space with them, attuned to their imaginative play, I stopped cleaning and lingered with their seemingly endless stream of ideas. Walker Percy stated, "To be aware of the possibility of the search is to be onto something."[3] When I saw their interest in making homes for squirrels, I realized that I was "onto something." Maxine Greene wrote that being onto something "involves a consciousness of what is not yet, of what might be; it is the 'more' we cannot predict."[4] My intuition and experience told me that the squirrel interest could open up possibilities for meaningful art making.

NARRATIVE SENSIBILITY

A sense of what is significant to children opens new and unexpected possibilities of what could happen in the curriculum.

When I observed the children engaged in making miniature worlds—what Edith Cobb[5] referred to as *Worldmaking*—I remembered the children's emotional energy around such activities in the past. They would work for hours, losing all sense of time. I had come to see these miniature worlds as stages or settings where children could create their own narratives or enact their own fictive dramas.

Over the years I found myself more attuned to the narrative potential of certain projects. I began listening *for* their stories, not just listening *to* their stories. Eudora Welty commented about this in her own context, writing:

> Long before I wrote stories, I listened *for* stories. Listening *for* them is something acutely more than listening *to* them. I suppose it's an early form of participation in what goes on. Listening children know stories are *there*. When their elders sit and begin,

---

3   Walker Percy, *The Moviegoer* (New York: The Noonday Press, 1960/1969), 13.
4   Maxine Greene, "Blue Guitars and the Search for Curriculum," in *Reflections from the Heart of Educational Inquiry: Understanding Curriculum and Teaching through the Arts,* eds. George Willis and William H. Schubert, (Albany, New York: State University of New York Press, 1991), 110.
5   Edith Cobb, 1977.

children are just waiting and hoping for one to come out, like a mouse from its hole.[6]

When the children engaged in Worldmaking, the stories were there; I anticipated them. When I encouraged Worldmaking, I was touching upon the significant. In addition to sensing the significant in the unstructured after-school space, I could give the children the type of attention Loris Malaguzzi described:

> What the child doesn't want is observation from the adult who isn't really there, who is distracted. The child wants to know that she is observed, carefully, with full attention…What is important to the child is that the teacher sees the child while the child is putting out the effort to accomplish the task—the processes are important, how the child is putting into the effort, how heroic the child doing this work."[7]

This brought to mind a time when Isabel and Rachel visited the after-school studio, and standing before their easels, began painting a picture of a special summer memory. Curious about how each of them approached their painting, I sat down to sketch and document how each painting unfolded. The girls were as interested in my sketches as they were in their own paintings. Rachel kept walking over to see what I had added. "I can't believe you are marking down every stroke we make," she said in a way that conveyed that my interest made her feel special. When they had finished, I had learned more about two different painting approaches to explore with children their age. The girls, I hoped, had a sense that I valued their efforts and their artwork.

NARRATIVE SENSIBILITY

Attentiveness to children's worldmaking and play allows new possibilities for blending the normative and narrative.

During the afternoon with the four children and the squirrel, I knew the children were aware of my presence, of my paying

---

6   Eudora Welty, *One Writer's Beginnings*, (Cambridge, MA: Harvard University Press, 1983), 14.
7   Malaguzzi, "Your Image of the Child: Where Teaching Begins," 55.

attention to their interests, and of my listening to their ideas. Every time they showed their work to their peers, they showed it to me as well. Had I seen only their final drawings, I would not have imagined all of the possibilities flowing from their work and our conversation. As Malaguzzi would say, when we observe children while they are engaged in a process, "we are opening a window and getting a fresh view of things. "Getting a fresh view of things" made it possible for me to see where the curriculum might go.

In the Reggio Emilia preschools, the metaphor of "tossing the ball" represents the emerging nature of their curriculum. Louise Cadwell wrote:

> A child is drawn to something and if we are listening, we notice. Then, perhaps, we want to play a game, so we "toss" them a twist, a provocation, a wide-open question about their idea. Then they respond with something marvelous that we did not anticipate, and the game continues. We don't know where the next ball will come from, but the game is fun and challenging for both child and adult, and we get better at playing it in many situations and scenarios.[8]

In Rachel's and Isabel's class, this is how the game of "toss the ball" unfolded. After I observed their interest in drawing squirrel homes and modeling them in clay, I introduced to their class the idea of investigating our school's backyard animals. The children and I went on a nature walk discovering squirrel homes, chipmunk burrows, and bird nests. Returning to the art room and working in pairs, the children created homes out of clay for the art room's collection of miniature woodland animal toys.

During our next art class, I invited them to create miniature squirrel families and three-dimensional, paper sculpture tree homes with pop-out animal friends. Again, the children caught the ball and tossed it back to me. On the day we added paper cylinders to make our tree drawings stand up, Melissa and Michelle cut out doors and began to construct

---

8   Louise B.Cadwell, *Bringing Learning to Life*, (New York: Teachers College Press, 2002).

beds, dressers, bathtubs, and televisions for the interiors. I invited them to share their ideas with the rest of the class, and when they did, their classmates immediately started to make their own interiors. Melissa and Michelle's ideas inspired Jerry to add a three-dimensional deck to the back of his tree house so his squirrel, who now wore a baseball cap, could lounge in the sun.

Jerry's idea inspired the whole class to "go three-dimensional" for the next two classes, adding decks, stairs, hot tubs, swimming pools, and playgrounds. The tree homes in Rachel and Isabel's class inspired the other three primary classes to create their own tree homes. And so, the game of "tossing the ball" not only included this class and myself, but other students and classes.

It did not stop there. Matthew came in during after school hours and designed a miniature bedspread and pillow for his squirrel. When I saw him drawing patterns on a piece of cloth for his bedspread and observed his friends looking on with interest, I invited his whole class to design quilted bed sets and weave rugs for their homes. Once again, they responded enthusiastically, catching the ball and tossing it back to me. Throughout the whole time, the children came in during their free time to play with their miniature squirrel worlds. The most popular theme was "our squirrels are having a sleepover." As I responded to the children's unfolding interests, we experienced together what Kieran Egan referred to as "uncovering" the curriculum.[9]

Preparing resources and materials and brainstorming possible ideas the moment I observed Rachel and Isabel's squirrel home interest allowed me to anticipate and make connections to the children as their ideas unfolded. I did not have a unit plan, but I had mapped out possible directions, waited, watched, prepared the environment, and remained open. According to Robert

NARRATIVE SENSIBILITY

Maintaining a narrative frame of mind, open to surprise and the unpredictable, uncovers the curriculum. Uncovering the curriculum can be done through a game of "tossing the ball."

---

9   Kieran Egan, *Teaching as Storytelling: An Alternative Approach to Teaching and Curriculum in the Elementary School* (Chicago, IL: University of Chicago Press, 1986).

Yinger *preparedness* is a frame of mind that keeps one open to surprise and the unpredictable. With this frame of mind,

> ...preparation acknowledges our limited ability to predict and the constructive nature of life. Preparation expects diversity, surprise, the random, and the wild. The work of preparing is getting ready, becoming equipped, and becoming receptive. The focus of preparation is on oneself not on a framework to constrain possibility. In a sense preparation enlarges the future.

Yinger contrasted preparedness to a more technical form of planning in which the teacher "seeks to deal with uncertainty by controlling the action and outcomes...to constrain the unpredictable, the random, and the wild."[10]

Following and responding to children's interests without having "unit plans" did not mean that I approached teaching with a laissez-faire attitude. In many ways, this emergent approach was more demanding and time consuming. Yet, it was also more fulfilling. My role was to: facilitate, guide, and prompt; prepare materials and the learning environment; design and propose possible projects; demonstrate skills and processes; introduce concepts. Sometimes I directed; sometimes I authored new ideas; sometimes I abandoned ideas, sometimes I played with the children, and sometimes I sat back and watched with sheer pleasure. I identified with Malaguzzi's description that

> ...the teacher must have the capacity for many different roles. The teacher has to be the author of a play, someone who thinks ahead of time. Teachers also need to be the main actors in the play, the protagonists. The teacher must forget all the lines he knew before and invent the ones he doesn't remember. Teachers also have to take the role of prompter, the one who gives the cues to actors. Teachers need to be set designers

---

10 Robert Yinger, "The Intelligence of Practice." In *Images of Reflection in Teacher Education,* eds. C. Waxman, Jerome Freiberg, Joseph C. Vaughan, and Marsha Weil, (Reston, VA: The Association of Teacher Education, 1988), 15.

who create the environment in which activities take place. At the same time, the teacher needs to be the audience who applauds.[11]

Having both structured art class time and less structured after-school time helped me to keep the narrative and normative in balance. During class time, I arranged experiences for learning skills, content, processes, and concepts,

NARRATIVE SENSIBILITY

Providing both structured and unstructured time and space allows for balancing the narrative and the normative.

based on the children's interests and passions. During after-school time, I listened closely to the children's self-initiated interests, and allowed these interests to inform the curriculum that I enacted during class time.

The unstructured space of the after-school studio opened other possibilities for keeping the pedagogical mobile in balance. In this unstructured space both the children and I could "linger" with their art.[12] Children were able to work according to their own rhythms, and I was able to remain attentive, gathering ideas for our next art project. In lingering, I found the truth of Wanda May's contention that to understand our students, we had to know them in contexts outside of the regular classroom, especially as they play.

The current emphasis on academics and standards has left little room for children's play. I believe it does not have to be an either-or situation. In *Miniature Worlds,* I saw once again how welcoming the narrative of children's play into the teaching and learning space opened up possibilities for me to reach my normative aims in ways that connected art more meaningfully to the children's lives. For example, one of my aims is for children to meet and work with real artists. Another is to collaborate with parents. When I invited the children to weave miniature rugs for their squirrels, I asked one of our parents, a weaver and spinner, to come and work with us. The children dyed

---

11 Malaguzzi, "Your Image of the Child: Where Teaching Begins," 56.
12 As I currently explore a more choice-based curricula, the after-school time of the self-initiated projects looks more like the art class time. See Katherine Douglas & Diane B. Jaquith, *Engaging Learners through Artmaking.* Teachers College Press, 2009.

wool in natural colors (to go along with our exploration of the colors of nature) and spun it into yarn on drop spindles. For many of them, it was their first weaving experience. Because they were weaving rugs for their own special squirrel there was a strong sense of engagement. If I had introduced weaving as an isolated unit plan, some children would have been interested, but some would not. As a fiber artist, I had been weaving with young children since they were in kindergarten. It was my desire for the young children—both boys and girls—to have positive experiences with weaving. Our squirrel exploration made this possible.

Another one of my normative aims is to connect the arts to the other subject areas in children's lives. Rachel's observation of the squirrel led to each of the four primary classes undertaking their own backyard animal exploration. One class was interested in a pop-out book, *Maisy's Playhouse*. Maisy, who was a paper doll mouse, lived in this playhouse book which when opened became her bedroom with a fold-out bed and quilt, a closet with hangers for her paper doll cut-out clothing, and doors that opened into her kitchen and bathroom. Seeing the children's interest in my paper dolls, and responding to their pleas to make their own, I invited them to first create their own backyard animal paper dolls and cut-out clothing. Because they had so many stories about their animals, I invited them to create books about their animals' lives. It just so happened that our school librarian had invited Jack Gantos, the children's book author, to visit our school. All of the primary classrooms were reading his *Rotten Ralph* animal book series. Meeting Jack Gantos at the same time that they worked on their own animal books was a powerful connection.

Another normative aim is for the children to have experiences responding meaningfully to works of art. It just so happened that earlier that year I had purchased a pop-out book of *Van Gogh's Bedroom*. It folded out the same way that Maisy's bedroom did. When I realized the connection, I introduced the children to Vincent van Gogh and his painting of his bedroom at Arles. Using both the pop-out bedroom and an actual art print of his bedroom, we had a meaningful interaction with this particular work of art. In another activity, the children imagined their squirrels walking into the art prints of tree paintings by artists such as Paul Signac, Vincent van Gogh, and Georgia O'Keefe. By asking which tree their squirrel would like for a home, the children entered into a lengthy, animated discussion in which they described and interpreted the paintings from the point of view of their squirrels, grounding their observations and preferences in the actual art works.

Throughout this time, between weekly art classes, the children continued to come in during after-school hours, playing with their animal characters and creating more ideas for their bedrooms. Craig, one of the kindergarteners, came in almost every day for *one and a half years* to create chapter books, extra rooms, and an extensive wardrobe for his animal, "Freddie the Turtle."

The quality of these experiences, according to Dewey, was *educative,*[13] because it had an agreeable influence on future experiences. These experiences also represent Dewey's notion of *continuity* in learning. Dewey maintained that continuity develops—first, because the experiences are grounded in the children's interests, and second, because the experiences connect past and present experience favorably to future experience.

Welcoming the children's play into the teaching-learning space allows me to see what matters most to them. Over the years I have come to see that the narrative—the children's play interests—have also become my normative aim. I now plan lessons that encourage and support their play interests. Through listening to the narrative, the narrative and normative have merged. I cannot not imagine being able to balance my pedagogical mobile without considering the children's interests in play. Whenever I ignore the children's play interests, the normative shapes carry too much weight. However, when I welcome them, all of the shapes weave and bob in a magically improvised performance.

---

13 Dewey, 1938.

CHAPTER 10

Art Classroom as Laboratory

CONNECTING WITH NATURE THROUGH THE ARTS

*If a child is to keep alive his [or her] inborn
sense of wonder...he [or she] needs the
companionship of at least one adult who can
share it, rediscovering with him [or her] the joy,
excitement and mystery of the world we live in.*

RACHEL CARSON

PEDAGOGICAL CONSIDERATIONS

In this chapter, I explore the notion of the art classroom as a laboratory. In her book *Young Geographers,* Lucy Sprague Mitchell illustrated how a classroom could be both an art studio and laboratory.[1] In this

---

1   Lucy Sprague Mitchell, *Young Geographers* (New York: Basic Books, 1934).

collaborative space, children can deepen their understanding of science concepts through art making.

At my laboratory school, primary science is taught in four and a half week blocks, alternated throughout the year with equally long blocks of social studies. Most teachers allot one to three hours a week to science lessons, each lasting from 30-60 minutes. At the primary level, the curriculum follows prescribed topics, but within those topics, teachers have complete freedom to determine the science content and the sequencing for the year. After the first nine weeks of school, typically the interns and student-teachers assume the teaching of science, in order to gain experience in planning units.

Alicia, a K-1-2 classroom teacher, described her usual science curriculum as teacher-directed and pre-determined, a combination of direct instruction and hands-on experimentation. She used hand-outs and worksheets as well as self-designed materials. For example, if the children were studying metamorphosis, the whole class might make similar egg carton caterpillars with pipe cleaners and googly eyes. Viewing her approach through the metaphor of a mobile, I thought science lessons were weighted toward the normative. Yet, as we began our collaboration, Alicia expressed an interest in creating more space for the children's voices.

When Alicia described the pressures in her context, I realized that balancing the narrative and normative could be a challenge. One of the pressures was teaching science to a class that contained both kindergarten and second grade students. Another pressure was the limited time for in-depth exploration of concepts during the four-and-a-half-week cycle. Fortunately, there would be three adults in the classroom (Alicia, Alicia's intern, and me). This allowed us to divide the class into three smaller groups so, that as necessary, we could work with the kindergarteners in a self-contained group. Further, the director of our department gave us permission to shape the primary curriculum by following the interests of the children at whatever pace we felt appropriate. Being able to construct the curriculum around the children's interests would give greater weight to the narrative.

In our collaboration, Alicia and I experimented with a social constructivist approach to learning, inspired by the practices of the Reggio Emilia preschools. As George Forman summarized, a social constructivist approach gives more voice to the narrative than a traditional teacher-directed approach. In this approach, the teacher invites the children to verbalize their initial theories, then to go through "a cycle of symbolization" where they externalize their ideas through different art media (e.g., drawing, clay), and then publicly share their meanings with others. Drawing helps the children think about the details of an event. Different art media help the children to deepen their understanding of an idea. The teacher encourages the children to dialogue with each other, to take on another's point of view, and to construct a group understanding of a topic. The teachers document the children's ideas to better understand how the children construct meaning.[2] Alicia and I believed this approach was appropriate given the children's ages and the importance of a "hands-on, minds-on approach" that emphasized nurturing the child's sense of wonder.[3]

The Apple Tree Project began during the first week of school when I took a small group of children outdoors to plant a perennial herb garden. On our way back to their classroom, the children exclaimed, "Look! There are apples everywhere!" The children looked up and saw an apple tree they hadn't noticed before. Excited by their discovery, they picked the apples off the ground and took them inside for their classmates to see.

Alicia and I realized that a wealth of possibilities existed in the children's interest. The previous year the children had pondered together the question, "Could we be 'friends' with the classroom newts and plants?" The children suggested that one way to express friendship was to take special care of them, making sure that they felt comfortable, happy, and loved. "Maybe the children would be interested in creating a friendship with the apple tree?" We could visit the tree throughout the seasons and explore the children's theories about change and life cycle—two topics required by the prescribed science curriculum. We could explore the children's interest in the ants, worms, and even birds that made the apple tree their home. We wanted the children to

2   George Forman. "The Project Approach in Reggio Emilia." In *Constructivism: Theory, Perspectives and Practice*, edited by Catherine Fosnot, 172-181. New York: Teachers College Press, 1996.

3   Susan J. Greishaber, and Carmel M. Diezmann, "The Challenge of Teaching and Learning Science with Young Children," in *Promoting Meaningful Learning*, ed. Nicola J. Yelland, (Washington, DC: National Association for the Education of Young Children, 2000), 90.

"experience" the tree through their senses and bodies and through an active engagement with different art media. Through these experiences, we hoped the children would come to a deeper understanding of how plants and animals live in relationship to each other. At the same time, we hoped we could nurture strong emotional bonds with the plants and animals in their lives.

The Apple Tree Project evolved as a year-long collaboration that blended the children's aesthetic ways of knowing (the narrative) with the prescribed science curriculum (the normative). A social constructivist approach addresses the notion of misconceptions. For all of the children, Alicia and I kept a large binder of their conversations, photographs of the children's work, and black and white reproductions of their drawings. In addition, we tape recorded and transcribed our conversations with the children so we could listen carefully to their interests and theories. If we saw the need, we could arrange learning experiences that invited children to revisit ideas. For the most part, we were more concerned that such young children would experience having wonderful ideas, rather than challenging every misconception.

As we reviewed these artifacts, we grouped them into five clusters— the apple tree in autumn; ants; the apple tree in winter; the apple tree in spring; earthworms. I drew from these clusters to portray a series of pedagogical enactments that began with the "discovery" of the apple tree in the fall and proceeded until the end of school in the spring.

VIGNETTE—THE APPLE TREE AND ITS FRIENDS

Pedagogical Enactment 1 – The Apple Tree in Autumn

To initiate a conversation with the children, Alicia and I prepared questions to ask them ahead of time. "Was it possible to be friends with a tree? If so, how could we show friendship? What are some things that could make our tree feel happy? Sad? Mad?" We also wrote down questions that enabled us to hear some of their initial theories. "Did trees have babies? Did our apple tree ever become hungry? Tired? Cold? What did it eat? Drink? Did it sleep? Dream?"

Sitting underneath the apple tree, I began the conversation with a group of eight second grade children by reminding them that at the end of the previous year they had said it was possible to be friends with their classroom pets and plants. "Was the apple tree a plant?" I asked. The children explained to me that it was, offering their reasons. I then asked, "Could we be friends with our apple tree? All of the children believed that we could and expressed a strong interest in being its friend.

> Jack: We could be friends by making sure we watered it. And maybe we could plant little trees around it so it could have many friends.
>
> Campbell: I have a favorite tree in my backyard. I leave it special messages and treats, especially when it is feeling sad. Maybe we could write messages to the apple tree."

"What would make our tree feel sad?" I asked.

> Jack: Maybe if someone carved stuff on it, it would hurt its skin.
>
> Campbell: If somebody cuts it down.
>
> Jonah: If you set its roots on fire.

"What would make our tree feel mad?" I continued.

> Mark: If you rip off all of its leaves.
>
> Max: If a beaver stuck its teeth in it, and it went timber and knocked into another tree.
>
> Jack: If you whack it. Szoom! Szoom! Szoom!"

The children continued to offer their theories about what our tree liked to eat and drink, how it made babies, if it dreamed while it slept, what made it happy. Woven into their responses was their continued fascination with the ants and worms in the apples on the ground in front of them. Before moving onto drawing the tree, many of the children played a movement game, imitating the tree's gesture with their bodies. Sitting down with clipboards and drawing materials, the children then drew from their observations of the apple tree's two trunks, its knobby bark, jagged leaves, and sour apples. Each drawing exemplified the children's focus on the apple tree's unique characteristics. For example, Dera, a second grader, portrayed the apple tree's slender and curvy intertwining trunks, textured bark, and leafiness (Figure 4). Anna, a new kindergarten student, captured its "apple-ness" (Figure 5).

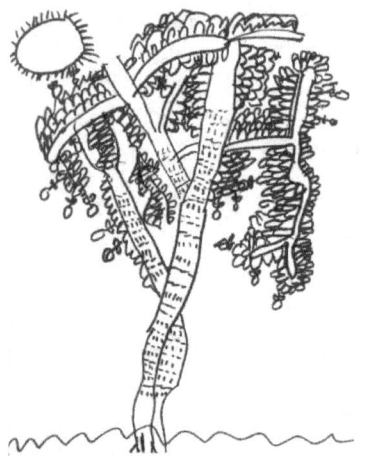

Figure 4. Dera's Drawing of the Apple Tree

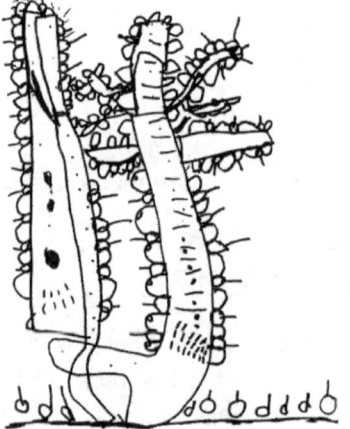

Figure 5. Anna's Drawing of the Apple Tree

Looking at the drawings, I saw how much their initial sensory and kinesthetic experiences enabled the children to draw this "particular" apple tree, rather than some generic lollipop version.

The Apple Tree in Clay

Knowing that each art medium has its own properties, Alicia and I wanted the children to become better acquainted with the tree through a variety of media. For instance, drawing the apple tree allowed children to express its leafiness and the apple-ness. Working in clay gave the children an opportunity to explore the tree's three-dimensionality, balance, and the relationship between the branches and the trunk.

Alicia's intern and I documented how each child approached the puzzle of balance—a developmental cognitive task that was both challenging and appealing to children of this age. Figure 6 illustrates the progression of the children's thinking from beginning to end. We also had a record of the children sharing their unique approaches with each other.

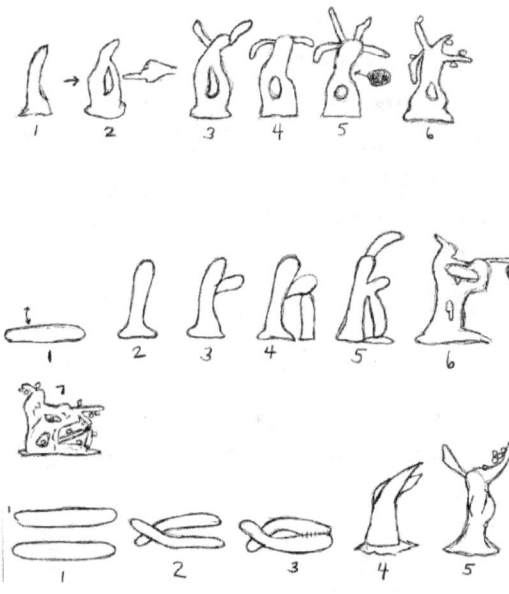

Figure 6. The Apple Tree in Clay

Each row shows the progression in clay by an individual child, beginning with "1," – showing how the child began in clay to make the apple tree, and ending with the higher number – showing the child's final creation. All of the sketches were completed by an adult observer documenting each child's process.

Drawing the Taste of Apples

Alicia and I wanted to explore the notion of "cross modal" drawing in which children represented their thinking across the senses or modalities, such as drawing the scent of an herb or representing the sound of rain. Alicia and I brought in six different kinds of apples, including our own tree's apples. We invited the children to taste each apple and then represent the taste. Through the use of non-representational lines, shapes, and colors, the children drew their experience of crunchiness, sourness, sweetness, sweet and sourness, juiciness, and "the best tasting apple in the world." For example, for a sweet tasting apple, one child chose a yellow marker and drew a long curvy and loopy-loop line. For a sour tasting apple, the same child chose a green marker and drew a long-jagged line. For the apple from our apple tree, the child chose her favorite color—pink—and drew a row of apples with a bite out of each. At the end of the row she drew a face with a huge smile and a hand rubbing its belly in delight. That drawing became for her "the best tasting apple in the world!"

Baby Apple Tree Theories

Following a conversation about the children's theories concerning how apple trees make baby apples trees, the children began drawing. This gave Alicia and me a way to explore their initial ideas about the tree's life cycle. The children tended to explain their theories in narrative form as they drew graphic representations of their thinking. Ellen's explained her theory as she drew the image in Figure 7:

> The cat eats an apple, and he has a seed in his stomach, and the seed comes out in his poo-poo.
>
> The seed goes down in the ground and the poo-poo covers it, and it grows into a small tree and then into a big tree.

Figure 7. Ellen's Drawing of her Baby Apple Tree Theory

Harvest Celebrations

As the children continued to observe the seasonal transformation of the apple tree, they prepared for a harvest celebration. Alicia and I invited them to print table clothes with apple and leaf motifs and to make applesauce from our tree's apples. We asked Rachel's dad to come in and share with the class about Succoth, the Jewish harvest celebration that many of our students enjoyed. Alicia and I told the children that for now, we would visit our tree throughout the fall, but in the winter, we would begin some new investigations. In the meantime, we were going to explore their interests in ants.

Pedagogical Enactment 2 – Ants

Throughout the fall the children maintained a strong interest in ants. One day they constructed a miniature world for them from dirt and other natural materials in the garden next to the apple tree. They molded a high mountain and sculpted passageways, tunnels, craters, and roads with twigs and stones for the "zillions of ants" they had discovered in the garden. Acknowledging their interest, Alicia and I proposed having our own ant farm in the classroom. The majority of the children responded enthusiastically, except two kindergarten girls who declared, "Bugs are yucky!"

While we waited for the ants to arrive for our ant farm, Alicia and I prepared the children by having an initial conversation with our three groups of eight. In each group, we invited them to share personal stories about experiences with ants. We then asked them to talk about what the world would look and feel like from an ant's point of view. My group immediately fell to the floor on their hands and knees, pretending to be ants. Rachel announced, "Everything looks giant and humongous from down here! This yellow marker looks like a huge wall." Giving them tiny pieces of paper and pens with tiny nibs, we asked the children to draw their initial theory of what an ant looks like. Most drew very simple ants; some with legs protruding from the abdomen; some with more than six legs (Figure 8).

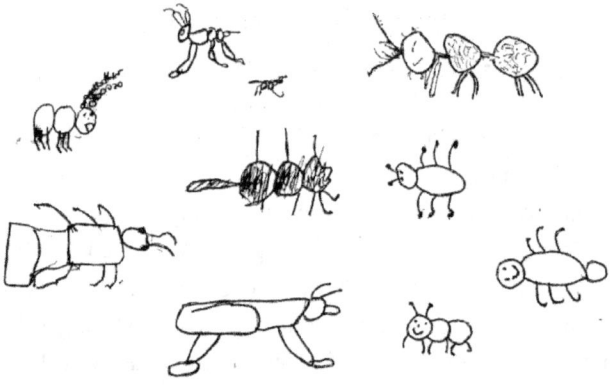

Figure 8. Initial Ant Drawings

When the ants for our ant farm arrived the following week, the children immediately became enthralled, even the two girls who thought bugs were yucky.

Max: Hey! They look like they're playing tag.

Lisa (observing them making tunnels in the sand): It looks like they are making the letters of the alphabet.

Considering where we should go next with this exploration, Alicia and I decided to ask the children, "If you could ask the ants anything you wanted, what would you ask them?" They were quick to respond. We kept their questions until later when we would discuss their theories for each question.

Max: Why is there no king in an ant colony?

Campbell: How do ants make babies?

Lisa: How do their tunnels stay open without collapsing?

Jack: How can they support themselves with such skinny legs?

Drea: How can they crawl on the ceiling of the ant farm and not fall off?

Mitch: How do they know when another ant is an intruder and not their own?

Analyzing our three initial conversations, we noted the children's interests in ant anatomy, social behavior, and life cycle. We began by investigating ant anatomy. Using magnifying glasses, the children studied the live ants, 3-dimensional models, and anatomical images of the ants' body parts and functions; in the process they acquired a vocabulary for describing their observations. After this initial immersion, the children drew their new theories of what an ant looked like, making visible their new understandings. Alicia and I were amazed at the children's new level of detail as we compared their new drawings to their initial ones. (We recorded the children's explanations.)

Figure 9. Jack

This is a fire ant. The head is shaped like an egg. The thorax and abdomen are very hairy. If you look at an ant with a magnifying glass, it has a lot of hair like this."

Figure 10. Kyle

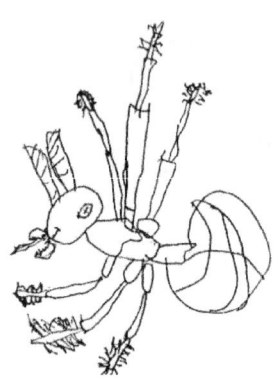

My ant is a red ant. Its abdomen looks like a basketball. Its head kind of looks like a raindrop. If you put its home on fire, they will put it out.

Figure 11. Campbell

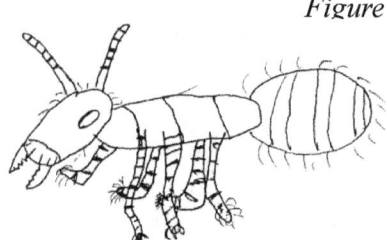

It's a black ant and the abdomen reminds me of the Easter egg I made last year. The thorax looks like my striped crayon.

From both a pedagogical and aesthetic point of view, Alicia and I believe the drawings gave far better insight into the children's understanding than handing out a photocopy of an ant in which they labeled the parts.

To deepen their understanding of ant anatomy, Alicia and I invited the children to work with a partner to create their ants in clay. Clay allowed them to think three-dimensionally about the relationship between body parts, such as where the legs are located in relation to the thorax or abdomen. Working in pairs allowed the children to draw upon each other's understandings to increase their own.

Ant Theories

Because some young children tend to look for "right answers" from adults or the authority of a book, we wanted them to express their ideas before researching their questions in the classroom library. To accomplish this, Alicia and I held another conversation with our small groups in which we returned to the questions the children had posed. How do ants dig tunnels without the tunnels collapsing?

> Max: Maybe they use spit to hold it in place.

> Drea: When a piece falls, they get it right away.

> Kyle (somewhat jokingly): Maybe the soldier ants use their guns.

How can ants tell each other apart?

> Jack: Because their antennas can sniff, and if they sniff someone who smells stinky, they know it's not a friend.

> Max agreed.

How are ant babies born? Can you draw your theory? As they worked, the children combined ideas of what they knew (e.g., eggs have yolks and humans deliver babies) with what they guessed might happen.

Figure 12. Max

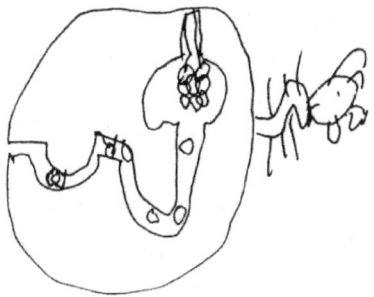

This is where the egg comes out. It starts up here, goes down the tube. This is where the yolk appears. Then the shell appears there like magic, and then it comes through the hole. After the queen lays the egg, it develops into things that wobble up and down. They're larva. It becomes a pupa or pupae, and then it grows into a baby ant. When it grows up, that's the life cycle, and it starts again.

Figure 13. Jack

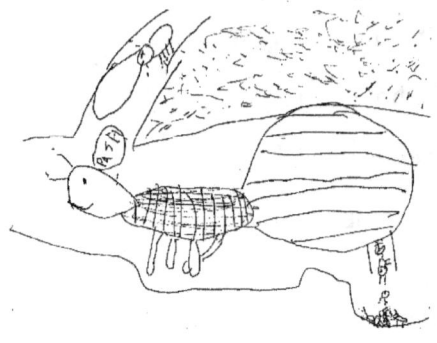

I think the ant squishes its way out of the tip of the queen's abdomen. It squeaks out. Squeak. Squeak."

Figure 14. Campbell

This is Mr. Beetle, and this is the queen, and she is laying all her little pupa things, and her workers are bringing her sugar. The pupae are lying on the bed. Mr. Beetle helps her squeeze the babies out. He's the doctor.

Because we were not able to acquire a queen ant and observe the life cycle process, the children researched their ideas in the classroom library during language arts. As a group, they were able to return to their visible theories and revise them.

Ant Facts and Fiction

Alicia and I discovered that when we created space for both the children's real and imagined art making, their interest in the ants as well as their emotional attachment to them seemed to deepen. In art class the children engaged in a series of activities:

- They constructed three-dimensional paper playgrounds for their ants.

- They drew underground homes and cities, combining ideas from both life and fantasy.

- They drew underground ant playgrounds, hospitals, restaurants, schools, and parks. They painted the ground on top of a clear piece of acetate so they could lift up the ground and peek under it to see their underground drawings.

As the children continued to research ants, Alicia and I proposed the idea of adapting a musical about ants for their scheduled class play. Working with the music and theater teachers, the children combined their research with elements of fantasy to create the performance, "Antics in Ant-sylvania."

The presentation of the play, the cast party with their parents and teachers, and the arrival of the holidays brought closure to our study of ants. I kept the ant farm stocked in my room throughout the year so the children and other classes could visit them at any time.

Pedagogical Enactment 3—The Apple Tree in Winter

When the children returned from holiday break, Alicia and I returned to the apple tree and had a conversation with the children about how the tree might be feeling—again appealing to their tendency to personify. We also asked them to share their theories about what might be happening inside the tree now that the weather was colder.

Many of the children felt that the tree was feeling lonely because it was cold, and because they couldn't visit it as much. They decided to create a mailbox for the tree in their classroom message center and write messages to cheer it up. I invited them to include a drawing that would make the apple tree happy. Kyle drew a snow fort around his picture of the tree. Campbell explained that a large sweater with many openings for branches and a bunch of winter scarves would make the tree happy and keep it warm. On the cover of her message, she drew a picture of the apple tree with five scarves wrapped around the branches (Figure 15).

Figure 15. The Cover of Campbell's Message for the Apple Tree

Inside, Campbell's message read:

Dear Apple Tree,

I miss you. I'm making you five scarves for five branches. I'm also making you a castle. You're the best apple tree in the world, and your apples make the best applesauce, and they are the best tasting apples too!

Love,

Campbell

PS. Are you a boy or a girl?

To make the tree feel less lonely, the children strung popcorn and cranberries to attract winter birds.

Alicia and I then asked, "What could we do to draw the children closer to the apple tree and keep them engaged?" I thought of past three-dimensional tree home projects, of Campbell's drawing of the scarves, of the upcoming change in the tree's appearance with spring in a few months. "Maybe the children would like to make a three-dimensional paper doll of the apple tree." I said. "They could draw the tree in winter and make winter clothing like Campbell's scarves. In the spring they could change its clothes to spring apple blossoms. In summer and fall, the tree's clothing of leaves could be changed again." When we proposed the idea to the children, they immediately embraced it.

The children drew the tree again, this time in winter. They created on its surface a patterned bark of neutral colors similar to colors they would find in nature in the winter. Then they created paper cut-out scarves, sweaters, hats, mittens, skates, sleds. They strung together burgundy and white glass beads to create cranberries and popcorn. They even wove scarves on miniature looms. When spring came, they created an outfit of spring apple blossoms. As the children played and acted out stories with their paper doll trees, Alicia and I continued to sense a deepening of the children's emotional connection to the tree.

Pedagogical Enactment 4 – The Apple Tree in Spring

The children thought of other ways to make the tree feel less lonely. They created bird sculptures out of clay to hang on its branches to keep it company and to welcome back the spring birds. In yet another conversation, the children shared their theories about migration and how birds find their way back to our school.

As spring grew closer and the apple tree's blossoms began to bud, Alicia and I invited the children to share their theories of how apple blossoms turned into apples. We picked off a few budding branches so that the children could experience the apple blossoms through their senses. The children had become even more focused in their observations and displayed a greater attention to details in their drawings (Figure 16).

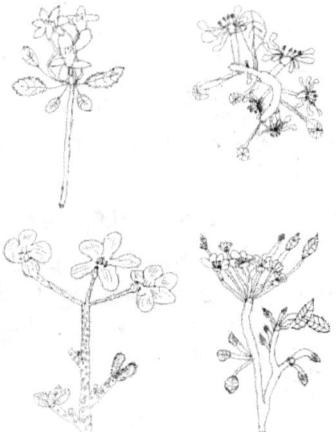

Figure 16. Four Observation Drawings of Apple Blossoms

The school year ended with planting a spring vegetable and sunflower garden. The children raised earthworms in their "earthworm hotel," and released them into the garden soil. The first graders and kindergarteners made sketchbooks as going away gifts for the second graders. They drew and painted apple blossoms for the sketchbooks, bringing closure to our yearlong study of the apple tree. On the last day of school, we said goodbye to the apple tree. We would be back in the fall to see if it had had a good summer.

BALANCING SENSIBILITIES

One of the sensibilities present in this collaborative context was the capacity and sensitivity to listen to both the children and to each other. Listening to the narrative required a *listening together*—a mutual, reciprocal listening. Baji Rankin defined collaboration as "the mutual guiding of the educational process by participants."[1] It was reciprocal and embraced a sense of community. Each participant was open to possibility and influenced the other. They each assumed the lead at different times.

Listening in this context required Alicia and me to be flexible, willing to embrace the unknown, and be comfortable with uncertainty. As Loris Malaguzzi noted, teachers have to be willing to "go with what might grow at that very moment both inside the child and inside [them] selves."[2] We had to try new ideas based on the children's interests and to be comfortable with the unexpected nature of life in the classroom.

Alicia and I created a "listening context"[3] in which we listened together to the children's

NARRATIVE SENSIBILITY

Collaborative, interdisciplinary pedagogy entails listening together with flexibility as well as embracing uncertainty and the unexpected.

---

1 Baji M. Rankin, *Collaboration as the Basis of Early Childhood Curriculum Development: A Case Study from Reggio Emilia, Italy* (Unpublished doctoral dissertation, Boston University, 1995), 34.

2 Loris Malaguzzi, "Your Image of the Child: Where Teaching Begins." *Child Care Information Exchange, 96* (1994): 53-54.

3 Rinaldi, "Documentation and Assessment," 81.

conversations, images, and ideas to "see learning through the children's eyes."[4] We mapped out possibilities ahead of time but remained open to what transpired in the classroom. Because this collaboration was a journey of learning for each of us, we did not always know what would happen next.

Listening with a narrative frame of mind meant listening to the children's aesthetic ways of making meaning, to their curiosities, to their theories, to how they represented their thinking in multiple languages. It required a willingness to document the children's learning through transcribing tape-recorded conversations, taking visual notes on how children approached a process (e.g., sketching the children's clay sculptures of apple trees), and reflecting on their symbolic representations. These visible traces of the children's thinking guided us in knowing what to do next.

In the collaboration, many possibilities opened as a result of our *welcoming the children's aesthetic ways of knowing* into the science classroom. In my reflections that follow, I refer to these possibilities as "a feeling for the organism" and "magic eyes."

A Feeling for the Organism

From the beginning of our collaboration Alicia and I wanted to teach science to children using an approach that valued their aesthetic ways of knowing. This meant creating a space for intuition, sensory-bodily knowing, play, curiosity, wonder, imagination, metaphor, visualization, emotional engagement, identification, personification, and what Malaguzzi referred to metaphorically as "the hundred languages"—*all* the multiple forms of symbolic representations, not only words and numbers.[5] We also wanted to create a space that invited the children to explore their natural world at a pace and rhythm that was congruent with their sense of time, not the compartmentalized time of a prescribed curriculum.

I knew that the arts had the power to engage the children emotionally with their subject matter. I had no idea that the children would become

---

4   Penny Oldfather, and Jane West, *Learning through Children's Eyes: Social Constructivism and the Desire to Learn* (Washington, DC: American Psychological Association, 1999), 77.

5   Malaguzzi, "No Way the Hundred Is There," 2-3.

as deeply engaged as they did. I was reminded of Evelyn Fox Keller's biography of the biologist Barbara McClintock whose work in maize and genetics won her a Nobel Prize. McClintock used the

> **NARRATIVE SENSIBILITY**
>
> Welcoming aesthetic ways of knowing promotes a "feeling for the organism."

language of affection, love, and kinship to describe her relationship to plants. Her language reflected a relational knowing, a sympathetic understanding, a somatic awareness:

> No two plants are alike. They're all different...I start with the seedling, and I don't want to leave it. I don't feel I really know the story if I don't watch the plant all the way along. So I know every plant in the field. I know them intimately, and I find it a great pleasure to know them.[6]

About McClintock's relationship to her plants, Keller wrote:

> Over and over, she tells us one must have time to look, the patience to "hear what the material has to say to you," and the openness to "let it come to you." Above all, one must have "a feeling for the organism."[7]

The children's words, responses, and visual representations of the apple tree and ants suggested to me that Alicia and I had created possibilities for the children to know the plants and animals in their lives more intimately. By beginning with our initial conversation on being friends with the apple tree and by asking questions that appealed to the children's natural tendency to personify, we created space for the children to develop emotional relationships with the subjects of study.

Both Judith Burton[8] and Victor Lowenfeld[9] suggest that children do not draw or paint objects in the world, they draw or paint their *relationship* with them. The initial exploration of the tree with our

---

6   Evelyn Fox Keller, *A Feeling for the Organism: The Life and Work of Barbara McClintock* (New York: W. H. Freeman & Company, 1983), 198.

7   Ibid.

8   Burton, 2000

9   Lowenfeld, 1957.

senses allowed the children to enter into a relationship and perceive its unique qualities. The more we encountered the tree through new drawing or sculpting experiences, the more differentiated the children's perceptions became; the more they attended to the tree's particular qualities. As Elliot Eisner wrote:

> To draw a tree...the artist must not only notice that the object to be drawn is a tree...but a *particular* tree...To do this, the artist must avoid the premature classification of schooling and instead remain open to the particular features...No tree, no oak tree, no young oak tree is the same as any other young oak tree. The task the artist faces is to experience individual features of *this* tree, of *this* person, and to create a form that succeeds in revealing the essential and unique features of the object seen.[10]

Vea Vecchi, a former atelierista at the Diana school in Reggio Emilia, Italy, stated that when she invites children to draw a natural object, she is not asking them to create a copy or reproduction of nature. She invites children to respond out of a relationship to the object and through this relationship capture the object's *identity*.[11] Building a relationship with the apple tree throughout the seasons of the school year enabled the children to capture its unique qualities, its *identity*. This knowing through the arts was intuitive, embodied, and somatic. Giving form to feeling opened possibilities for children to acquire, in their own way, a firsthand *feeling for the organism*. It also invited children to see their world with *"magic eyes,"* as illustrated in the story that follows.

Seeing with Magic Eyes

Author Tom Hughes recounted a conversation with his daughter, Caitlin:

---

10 Elliot W. Eisner, *The Kind of Schools We Need* (Portsmouth, NH: Heinemann, 1998), 63.
11 Vea Vecchi, *The Theatre Curtain*. Paper presented at the Children, Spaces, and Relations Conference, Cyert Center for Early Childhood Education, Pittsburgh, PA, 2000.

When my daughter Caitlin was younger, we were walking by the docks near where we live. It was difficult for me to spend as much time with her as I would like because of my work, so the little time I had with her was precious. In an effort to use the time well I asked her what she saw as we approached the fishing boats which had recently returned from a trip.

I had expected her to say, "I see the fishing boats," but that is not what she said.

She said, "I see the white tops of the waves as they enter the harbor…that is their way of saying hello to the shore. And I see the wind which the seagulls ride on…sometimes it is blue but today it is pink. And I see men in the fishing boats…they are like fish who became men but wanted to stay on the sea, except for one—he is a walrus."

Caitlin continued, but already I had heard so much more than I could hold, and I needed more time to appreciate all that she saw. I asked her how it was she could see all this because all I saw were the fishing boats, and she replied, "I have magic eyes." [12]

Jerome Bruner reminded teachers that real scientists rely on physical intuition, metaphorical thinking, and narrative knowing. Science—as often taught in schools—does not mirror the quirky, non-rational world of working scientists. In his proposal of the *spiral curriculum*, Bruner argued that "any subject can be taught to any child at any age in some form that is honest." Citing Margaret Donaldson, he maintained that "a child who has a good, intuitive grasp of a domain at one stage of development leads

NARRATIVE SENSIBILITY

Narrative pedagogy allows time and space for seeing with "Magic Eyes."

---

12 Quoted in Patrick Fahey, "Magic eyes: Transforming Teaching through First Grade Sketchbooks," *Visual Arts Research* 22, no. 1 (1996): 34.

to better, earlier, and deeper thinking in the next stage when the child meets challenging new problems in that domain." [13]

Bruner had observed that young children represent their intuitive understandings of science in the form of narrative. Ellen and her classmates' narrative depictions of their theories about how the apple tree made baby apple trees was natural and appropriate for their age. Alicia and I wanted to keep the children's narrative depictions alive. We saw that by second grade many children resorted to labeling their pictures with arrows and diagrams. We knew that they would be exposed to this system of heuristics throughout most of their schooling, and it had its place at the right time. Choosing to develop their narrative, intuitive ways of seeing and being in the world in the early years was for Alicia and me one way of cultivating "magic eyes."

Karen Gallas has noted that often students who show little interest in science may be labeled as "having no aptitude" for it. She discovered, however, that any subject could come alive for students through a "personal, imaginative contact."[14] Alicia told me that before we began to collaborate, some of her students claimed they did not like science. As the children began to become engaged through their imagination—their magic eyes—both students and their parents shared with her their enthusiasm. By the end of the year, the two kindergarten girls, who initially did not like tiny creatures, caringly picked up the classroom earthworms and allowed them to crawl all over their hands—with delight and wonder.

Max van Manen cautioned that children's natural curiosity and wonder about their worlds can be stopped when adults see a child's question as something that needs a quick and simple answer instead of trying to support the child's natural inclination to *live* the question. When young children ask, "What is that?" they are looking for an adult to converse about the world; they are asking for time to dialogue, time to think, to wonder, to marvel." Yet adults often respond with a label for an object, which is different, van Manen contended, from naming. "Naming something is getting to know what that thing really is, what it

---

13 Jerome Bruner, *The Culture of Education* (Cambridge, MA: Harvard University Press, 1996), 119, 120.
14 Karen Gallas *Imagination and Literacy (*New York: Teachers College Press, 2003), 75.

is in its *whatness* and *thatness*."[15] When Alicia and I chose not to read any books on the apple tree's life cycle until after the children developed their own theories, we supported them in *living* the questions. When we invited the children to create questions to ask the ants, we cultivated their ability to *live* the questions. When we explored a subject in depth over a period of time at the child's pace, we also offered a way for children to *live* the questions.

Often the children began an exploration with much excitement and curiosity. We wondered, however, if their interest could be sustained over the whole school year as other interests vied for their attention. Tactful teachers, van Manen contended, keep alive the interests that inspire children's initial questions. Taking this responsibility to heart, we saw ourselves as "animators." In his book, *The Grammar of Fantasy*, Gianni Rodari described an animator as one "who brings to life creative play across all subjects of the curriculum and all realms of the imagination." Schools should be "cooperative, imaginative learning communities" where teachers and children engaged collaboratively in imaginative play.[16] Gallas expressed a similar idea when she described teachers and children in "collaboration as imaginators."[17] Herbert Kohl, in his introduction to Rodari's book, reminded teachers that a grammar of imagination invites the children to see "the possibilities of things" and to confront everyday experience with the question, "What if?"[18]

In our art-science collaboration, "what if" questions animated our conversations with the children. For instance—What if an apple tree had feelings; what if an apple tree could be your friend; what if an apple tree wore winter clothes; what if an apple tree was lonely; what if ants had underground cities like humans; what if you could see the world from the viewpoint of an ant.

Louise Cadwell advised adults to see young children's imaginative, poetic, and metaphoric use of language to describe their world as "their

---

15 van Manen, *The Tone of Teaching*, 38, 40.
16 Gianni Rodari, *The Grammar of Fantasy: An Introduction to the Art of Inventing Stories* (New York: Teachers and Writers Collaborative, 1996), ix.
17 Gallas, 63.
18 Kohl, Herbert. Forward. In *The grammar of Fantasy: The Art of Inventing* Stories, edited by Gianni Rodari, ix-xi. New York: Teachers & Writers Collaborative, 1996.

own special intelligence instead of thinking it is cute and/or incorrect."[19] It is this unique way of seeing and being that enable children to see their world through "magic eyes."

In our collaboration, Alicia and I could listen together to the narrative and the normative. If Alicia or I gave too much weight to the normative, we brainstormed alternatives. Through our mutual listening, we could give each other feedback to create a sense of equilibrium in the classroom.

---

19 Louise B. Cadwell, *Bringing Learning to Life* (New York: Teachers College Press, 2002), 66.

CHAPTER 11

Cultivating Aesthetic Sensibilities

A DELICATE BALANCE

*...the way people live their lives is in itself an artistic
process; as the artist takes materials composing them
into a workable aesthetic so do we take disparate parts
of our lives, the daily rituals, friendships, transitions,
and moments and put them into balance.*

MARY CATHERINE BATESON

A s an art teacher, I see my teaching as an artistic process. Daily I seek to compose into a workable aesthetic all the disparate parts of my teaching life—the art lessons, classroom rituals, relationships with children, transitions—and put them into balance. I have likened my teaching to a mobile. As the teacher-artist, I rely on my sensibilities to balance the narrative and normative shapes in varying configurations to bring aesthetic satisfaction for both the children and myself.

Elliot Eisner wrote that teaching is an art "guided by educational values, personal needs, and by a variety of beliefs and generalizations that the teacher holds to be true."[1] Teachers like artists do not abide by prescriptions; they respond to the qualities that unfold during the course of a lesson; they shift their aims in process; they orchestrate activities to engage children in intrinsically satisfying learning experiences—experiences which can be characterized as aesthetic.

In this chapter, I share how I view the narrative sensibilities discussed in the preceding chapters through an aesthetic lens. I cluster these "aesthetic sensibilities" as aesthetic vision, a rightness of fit, improvising the dance of shapes, holding onto tensions, imagining and playing with possibilities, and experiencing aesthetic satisfaction.

Aesthetic Sensibility—Aesthetic Vision

The phrase *aesthetic vision* came to me when I read Anne Sullivan's article, "Notes from a Marine Biologist's Daughter: On the Art and Science of Attention." I was immediately drawn to the title, most likely because of my growing interest in children's explorations of art and nature through the collaboration with Alicia. Sullivan referred to a heightened level of consciousness about what one perceives as "aesthetic vision."

> Aesthetic vision engages a sensitivity to suggestion, to pattern, to that which is beneath the surface as well as to the surface itself. It requires a fine attention to detail and form: the perception of relations (tensions and harmonies); the perception of nuance (colors of meaning); and the perception of change (shifts and subtle motions). It dares to address the effable.
>
> Teachers who function with aesthetic vision perceive the dynamic nature of what is unfolding in front of them at any given moment.[2]

---

1   Elliot W. Eisner, *The Educational Imagination* (New York: Macmillan, 1979), 153.
2   Anne Sullivan, "Notes from a Marine Biologist's Daughter: On the Art and Science of Attention," *Harvard Educational Review* 70, no. 2 (2000), 220-221.

I pondered Sullivan's text word for word and asked, "What did these sensibilities mean in my context?" I began with ...

A sensitivity to suggestion. When Ben drew a picture and showed it to me, he was suggesting that I notice and pay attention. How did I respond to this suggestion? Anna came in during after-school hours and wanted to paint at the easel. Did I read this as a suggestion to explore her interest in more depth in the future? When I saw a group of children drawing my beta fish and underwater castles or when I saw princesses and dragons drawn in a majority of sketchbooks, did I pay attention to these suggestions for possible curricular explorations? When Derek and Bobby took their sketchbooks under the table to draw, were they suggesting that I needed to have more private spaces in the art classroom?

A sensitivity to pattern. Was I paying attention to the child who repeatedly got frustrated? Were there students who responded enthusiastically every time I brought out clay? What drawing themes did individual children repeat in their work?

A sensitivity to that which is beneath the surface as well as to the surface itself. What emotions were conveyed behind Sarah's expression? What meaning was being conveyed in Tim's drawing of an airplane crash?

A perception of relations (tensions and harmonies). Was I aware of children's friendships? Did I sense when things were going smoothly and when they were not? Did I recognize a tension when I saw it and withhold my knee jerk reactions? Was I aware of the moods of individual children and the atmosphere of a class?

A perception of nuance (the colors of meaning) Was I aware of the subtle suggestions of tone of voice, body gestures and posture, of unspoken words, of facial expressions? Did I pick up on these qualities as a lesson unfolded?

A perception of change (shifts and subtle motions). Did I perceive changes in mood? In interests? In children's attention? Was I aware of how the weather, the time of day, the season, and the holidays influenced the students? Was I aware of the subtle changes in the mobile when the narrative and normative shapes began to shift?

A perception of the dynamic nature of what was unfolding. Was I aware of how the narrative and normative shapes on the mobile were interacting with each other? What was happening when I brought a pet into the classroom? What was happening when I introduced a new material? What was happening when Jerry made his squirrel deck, and everyone wanted to make one?

Aesthetic vision calls my attention to particulars; it is a sensibility that is essential for tacit knowing.

While Aesthetic Vision focuses my attention on particulars, the sensibility of Rightness of Fit helps me to see the particulars in relation to the whole. They allow me to intuit the gestalt.

Aesthetic Sensibility—The Rightness of Fit

Rightness of Fit guides me in being attuned to individual children while attending to the larger classroom patterns. Calder took disparate elements and composed and balanced them into a configuration that pleased him. He let all of the elements speak to him as he balanced them. When asked how he knew where to place a shape or balance a wire, he responded, "In his bones he knew right from wrong."[3] The sensibilities encompassed in *rightness of fit* let me know in my bones when the pedagogical mobile is balanced or out of kilter.

When I am guided by a *rightness of fit*, I see all of the shapes in relation to the whole. I see which ones need to be adjusted. Maybe it is my normative lesson plan; maybe the narrative shape is too large, and I have to balance it with a normative shape that is larger, or maybe I have to adjust the center of balance on the tension rod so that the narrative or normative receive more weight. Over time, I have cultivated a reservoir of embodied knowledge by attending to details and then forming holistic intuitions. As Rudolph Arnheim asserted, "Intuition supplies us with the overall structure of a situation and determines the place and function of every component within the whole."[4]

As Eisner noted, when artists are working on a painting, ceramic sculpture, or a mobile, they are "composing qualitative relationships

---

3 Throughout this chapter, my references to Calder are drawn from Jean Lipman's book, *Calder's Universe*, (Philadelphia, PA: Running Press Book Publishers, 1976).

4 Rudolph Arnheim, "The Double-edged Mind: Intuition and the Intellect," in *Learning and Teaching the Ways of Knowing* ed. Elliot W. Eisner,77-96 (Chicago, IL: University of Chicago Press, 1985), 82.

that satisfy some purpose." Organizing the qualities does not depend on rules, formulas, or prescribed guidelines. Making adjustments depends on attention to nuance—the texture of materials, the value of colors, the position of elements. As Nelson Goodman put it, "One knows when one is right because one feels the relationships. One modifies one's work and feels the results."[5] Art educational historian, Diana Koreznik, suggested, teachers, like artists, are guided by their sense of the whole:

> Out of all the complexity that is art making, the teacher shapes a lesson, something derived from the teacher's own personal educational history, knowledge of the needs of children, constraints of schools, and knowledge of the field of art.[6]

Aesthetic Sensibility—Improvising the Dance of Shapes

Calder's mobiles are often referred to as a dance of shapes—"any air current would set the parts moving within a pattern to create a constantly shifting dance in space." He himself used the analogy of dance when talking about his mobiles. Calder said, "I want to use the motion for its contrapuntal values as in good choreography."[7] Art historians and critics have remarked that his mobiles are "unpredictable and ever changing" and "more truly alive than any other man-made thing."[8] His work is described as innovative, fresh, interesting, original. He was said to have taken sculpture off the museum pedestal and pushed it beyond traditional definitions. The British painter Ben Nicholson wrote:

> ...the mobile turned slowly in the breeze...turned slowly in and out, around, above, and below one another, with their shadows chasing, round the white walls in an exciting interchanging movement, suddenly

5   Elliot W. Eisner, "What Can Education Learn from the Arts about the Practice of Education?" *Journal of Curriculum and Supervision,* 18, no. 1 (2002), 8-9.
6   Maurice Brown, and Diana Koreznik, *Art Making and Education* (Chicago, IL: University of Chicago Press, 1993), 197.
7   Lipman, *Calder's Universe,* 172.
8   (Janson, 1986, p. 740).

> hastening as they turned corners and disappearing—
> it was alive like the hum of the city, like the passing
> river, but it was not a work of art—imprisoned in a
> gold frame or stone-dead pedestal in one of our marble-
> pillared mausoleums. It was "alive" and that, after all,
> is not a bad qualification for a work of art.[9]

Calder himself was never certain how the mobiles would behave when "the wind struck them with their dancing movements." He remarked, "Oh, I know pretty well what will happen, but it's all 'cut and try,' and sometimes they surprise me."[10] Calder relied on chance relationships. He wanted random, less predictable motion. He valued the elements of chance and spontaneity.

David Perkins used the concept *mobility* to describe the teacher's ability to make intuitive judgments as the lesson unfolded.[11] This notion of mobility fits well with my metaphor of the mobile. As the pedagogical mobile moves, I need to balance the narrative and normative. While everything is in flux, I need to be flexible and move with the direction of the students, with the unfolding of my lesson, with the flow of my intuition. When the normative and narrative shapes begin to shift into new configurations, I need to be able to make rebalancing adjustments *as they happen* and *throughout* the lesson. Dewey referred to this as *flexible purposing*. Drawing upon Calder's work, I call it *improvising the dance of shapes*.

These improvisational sensibilities relate closely to the intuitive sensibilities of the *rightness of fit* because both rely on an awareness of the unfolding qualities in a lesson. Both rely on embodied knowing. Whereas *rightness of fit* relies on seeing relationships and having a feel for them, these sensibilities rely more on improvisational thoughtfulness, which van Manen explained was the embodied skill of instantly knowing how to interpret ever changing situations.[12] It requires an intuitive sense of timing. It is the ability to respond innovatively in

---

9 Richard G. Tansey, and Fred S. Kleiner, eds., *Gardner's Art through the Ages, 2nd ed.*, (New York: Harcourt, Brace & Company, 1996), 1064-65.

10 Lipman, *Calder's Universe*, 265.

11 David N. Perkins, "Creativity by Design," *Educational Leadership* 42, no. 1 (1984):18-25.

12 van Manen, *The Tact of Teaching.*

the face of the unpredictable, to be flexible and change one's plans when the situation calls for it.

Eisner stated that teaching was an art because often "the ends it achieves are created during the process."[13] In education, the ends are often stated first, such as in behavioral objectives, and then the means for reaching the objectives are planned, implemented, and then evaluated. In contrast, in the artistic process,

> ...[the] ends shift; the work yields clues that one pursues, in a sense, one surrenders to what the work in process suggests.[14]

Artists respond to the qualities in a work of art as they unfold; they are responsive to what the materials tell them; they are in dialogue. They might start out with an idea, but as they work with materials and respond to the unfolding qualities, their aims change. Barrie Barrell, in his article *Classroom Artistry*, clarified that flexibility is not the same as disorganization:

> The teacher who takes advantage of the sudden appearance of the rainbow to shift the focus of a writing lesson, or who decides to combine the writing lesson with a science lesson on prisms, is exercising Perkin's notion of mobility, not any lack of organization. The teacher is taking advantage of a particular teaching moment and not teaching on a whim.[15]

Aesthetic Sensibility—Holding the Tension of Opposites

When Calder created his mobiles, he balanced the wires on his fingers until he gradually worked out their equilibrium. Finding the center of balance depended on the size, weight, and angle of the shapes. Calder enjoyed working with opposites and having them exist side by side in a state of dynamic tension. He contrasted light and dark colors,

---

13 Eisner, The Educational Imagination, 154.
14 Eisner, "What Can Education Learn from the Arts," 10.
15 Barrie Barrell, "Classroom Artistry," *The Educational Forum, 55*, no. 4 (1991), 337.

organic and geometric shapes, vertical and horizontal lines. Calder was a master at holding the wires between opposing elements in tightrope tension.

Just as creating tensions in a work of art is desirable to the artist, Palmer maintained that holding tensions among opposites—practicing paradox in teaching— "creates an electric charge that keeps us awake."[16] Paradox pushes us into a frame of mind of heightened awareness.

Welcoming paradox into teaching means rejecting "either-or" thinking and embracing the "both-and." Palmer suggested, for example, that classroom space can be both open and bounded, hospitable and "charged," inviting the voice of the individual and the voice of the group. Teaching art to young children is filled with tensions—between listening both to the individual child and to the whole class; between allowing for unstructured and structured time; between standing back to allow things to unfold and to offering direction; between setting boundaries and allowing for free expression; between expectations in private versus public places; between creative self-expression and mutuality/collaboration; between planning and improvisation.

Here are additional tensions I encountered:

Did I let the children copy a friend's idea or not?

Did I let them digress from the classroom project and explore their own interest or not?

Did I demonstrate a technique or let them discover it first?

Did I let them struggle for a while with a problem or did I offer assistance—and if so, when?

Did I let the child work alone when everyone else was working in pairs?

Did I show teacher and student examples of a project or not?

Did I ignore a tantrum or lift the child on my lap?

There are no rules or absolute answers to such questions. Every situation requires a reading of the child, the context, the activity, the time of day, my past experiences with the child, my mood, the child's

16 Palmer, 74.

mood, my normative aims, the amount of time available, the presence of the other children. As Palmer reminds me, holding the tension of opposites is done by *being*, not doing. The wire holding tensions is balanced by the sensibility of intuition—my sense of what seems the right fit for that moment.

Palmer maintained that our culture and our schools emphasize objective, analytic ways of knowing; we learn to see "everything as this or that, plus or minus, on or off, black or white; and we fragment reality into an endless series of *either-or's*. In a phrase, we [think] the world apart."[17] Regrettably, as art educator Ron Neperud pointed out, we in art education all too often succumb to this tendency to polarize— we polarize the child and the subject, modernist and postmodernist approaches, fine arts and crafts, individual self-expression and community.[18] Encouraging teachers to "love the contradictions," Palmer quoted Rilke's *Letters to a Young Poet*. "Be patient toward all that is unresolved in your heart and try to love the questions themselves."[19]

Aesthetic Sensibility—Imagining and Playing with Possibilities

Calder was known for his prolific ability to invent new ways of using materials and objects. Writing about Calder's mobiles, Jean Paul Sartre said, "They have too many possibilities and are too complex for the human mind, even their creator, to predict the combinations."[20] In both personality and art, Calder was known for his playful, childlike qualities. At the heart of Calder's work was "the circus esthetic"— "a combination of suspense, surprise, spontaneity, humor, gaiety, playfulness." Calder had once said, "To keep one's art young, one must imitate animals. What do they do? They play."

In his book, *Playgrounds of the Mind*, John Barrel posited that "playing with ideas" lies at the heart of the creative process. Both the

---

17 Palmer, 83, 62.
18 Ron W. Neperud, "Transitions in Art Education: A Search for Meaning," in *Context, Content, and Community in Art Education: Beyond Postmodernism*, ed. Ron.W. Neperud (New York: Teachers College Press, 1995), 1-22.
19 Rainer Maria Rilke, *Letters to a Young Poet*. (translated by Mary D. Herter Norton). (New York: Norton, 1993), 35.
20 Sartre quoted in Lipman, 229.

child and adult mind can "play an infinite variety of roles, enact myriad possible courses of action, resolve scores of problems, toy with ideas.[21]

Indeed, Cobb asserted the adult imagination has its foundation in the play of the child.[22] Louis Rubin in his book *Artistry in Teaching,* stated that one of main characteristics of artistic teachers is their capacity to be imaginative.[23] George Szeleky wrote that our childhood interests in play influence who we are as adult artists, and I would add, who we are as art teachers.

In a narrative frame of mind—when I am in touch with my own childhood and the children's; when I make space for the children's way of being in the world—play is an inevitable and essential quality of our shared art experience.

In the chapter, *Art Classroom as Laboratory,* I mentioned Gianni Rodari's view of the teacher as an "animator"—someone who brings to life creative play and imagination in the classroom and across the curriculum. Herbert Kohl described this role in more detail:

> The teacher creates imaginative challenges for children,
> speaks with children about what they are doing, listens
> carefully to what the children say, and follows their lead
> in the development of projects. The teacher is not just
> a facilitator or coach. On the contrary, the teacher is an
> active participant who brings exercises and ideas to the
> learning situation, challenges the children to think and
> speak about what they are doing. This inspiring vision
> of teacher as artist and visionary walks the delicate line
> between didactic and hands-off teaching.[24]

Imagining possibilities also relates to *my image of the child.* In *The Tact of Teaching,* van Manen said, "To see the child, is to see possibility."[25] Marilyn Zurmuehlen citing Martin Buber, shared the story about a new teacher who realized that, though he did not choose

21 John Barrel, *Playgrounds of Our Minds* (New York: Teachers College Press, 1980), 3.
22 Cobb, 1977.
23 Louis J. Rubin, *Artistry in Teaching* (New York: Random House, 1985).
24 Herbert Kohl, "Forward," In *The Grammar of Fantasy: The Art of Inventing* Stories, ed. Gianni Rodari, (New York: Teachers & Writers Collaborative, 1996), x.
25 van Manen, *The Tact of Teaching,* 1.

his students, "he *can* choose how he thinks about them. He chooses to think beyond what they appear to be at the moment to what they can become."[26]

Seeing possibilities is essential for enacting a narrative pedagogy. It means that I look beyond my superficial interpretations, my feelings of annoyance or frustration, and my fixed ideas. The sensibilities associated with *aesthetic vision* are closely aligned with seeing possibilities and being open to transformation. As an artist-teacher, I must perceive "the potential for transformation within any apparent fixity—a block of wood, a piece of clay, a display of words, the configuration of a classroom, or the behavior of an individual child."[27]

Singer and Singer[28] found that positive emotions such as joy, liveliness, and excitement accompanied the make-believe play of the young child. Imagining possibilities contributes to the sensibility of *aesthetic satisfaction*.

Aesthetic Sensibility—Experiencing Aesthetic Satisfaction

According to Lipman, Calder expressed in his art "his sense of pleasure and joy of life. His life, in all media, ha[d] a core of pure joy, in the concept, the execution, the color—all of which directly communicate[d] pleasure to the viewer." [29] When Calder showed his work in museums, "rarely did one see a gallery more alive, more boisterous, more joyful—and more visitors amused."

In the Reggio schools where creativity and aesthetic satisfaction are valued, a maxim guides the school—*Niente Senza Gioia*—Nothing Without Joy. Loris Malaguzzi said, "I believe that children expect from adults the capacity to offer joy. They ask it of everyone and everything. Without truly radiating and receiving joy, an adult cannot foster an atmosphere where children can invent or create"[30]

---

26 Zurmuehlen, *Studio Art*, 32.
27 Sullivan, 221.
28 Singer, Dorothy, and Jerome T. Singer. *The House of Make-believe: Children's Play and the Developing Imagination.* Cambridge, MA: Harvard University Press, 1990.
29 Lipman, 279, 32.
30 Malaguzzi quoted in Goleman, Kaufman, and Ray, 1992, p. 83.

The anthropologist Ellen Dissanayake pointed out, "Certainly pleasure and satisfaction may accompany our forgetting or escaping the care and trivialities of practical daily life and vicariously experiencing the shapely, economical, beautiful, integrated properties that characterize aesthetic as compared to ordinary properties."[31] It is important not to view joy and pleasure as trivial. As Amy Giles stated, meaningful art experiences for young children embody intensity and purpose. She defined intensity as *pleasure, enjoyment,* and *attention.* Working with materials provides deep satisfaction for young children. To transform materials into forms requires focus and concentration. It is possible for children to be so deeply engaged that they wonder where the time has gone. During these times, children do not want to leave; often they return and work for hours. John Dewey said that art experiences that consume you lead you to want more.

When the children are deeply involved with the process of making art, a palpable sense of joy, pleasure, and deep satisfaction permeates the classroom atmosphere—for the children and me. The notion of both the adult and children experiencing aesthetic pleasure is an essential aspect of enacting a narrative pedagogy. Krechevsky and Stork, writing about Reggio Emilia preschools said:

> Creating or finding experiences that will stimulate excitement, curiosity, and joy in children *and adults* is a fundamental part of teaching in the Reggio view. Reggio teachers strive to provide materials and experiences (e.g., posing riddles, immersing materials in light, dressing up in imaginative costumes) that will generate feelings of surprise, amusement, wonder, and even betrayal.[32]

They went on to say that in the Reggio learning communities, teachers "nurture their own capacities to feel amazement, passion, and a sense of adventure." Certainly, this has been the case for me. When

---

31 Ellen Dissanayake, *What is Art For?* (Seattle, WA: University of Washington, 1988), 66.
32 Mara Krechevsky, and Janet Stork, "Challenging Educational Assumptions: Lessons from an Italian-American Collaboration," *Cambridge Journal of Education,* 30, no.1 (2000), 70.

I am creative, playful, passionate about a lesson, and derive joy from my interactions with the children, I am better able to create learning experiences where the children derive pleasure as well. To prepare the learning space for the aesthetic, I have to be in touch with my own source of creativity and satisfaction. As John Dewey said, to see the aesthetic we have to move out of the humdrum and boredom.

When I linger with the children as they engage in intrinsically satisfying art making, I remain attuned to their interests, ideas, and emotions. In turn, I am able to balance the pedagogical mobile so it "dances with the joy of life."

Cultivating Narrative and Aesthetic Sensibilities

As I read about Calder's life, I gained a sense of how his aesthetic sensibilities developed over time. As a young child, Calder spent hours in his studio inventing miniature toys. As an adult, his early training was in mechanical engineering. However, when engineering no longer appealed to his aesthetic sensibilities, he left the field and pursued art. He had always been interested in creating sculptures that moved, even as a child. His first moving sculptures were hand motorized. With time, the hand-motorized sculptures were less satisfying to create, and he began to design mobiles that were self-supporting and suspended from the ceiling, opening for him possibilities to explore movement and balance in infinite configurations. Over the years his mobiles became more intricately balanced, and he took on greater challenges. He derived great satisfaction from his work.

Reflecting on his earlier and then later work revealed to me how his aesthetic sensibilities deepened throughout his life. He relied less on sketches and technique and more on intuition. His growth as an artist was similar to the growth of many teachers. Teachers have had early experiences which have inspired them to go into the field of teaching, receive training in the techniques and methods of instruction, and then over time embody their teaching so deeply that they are able to discard mechanical methods for more authentic curriculum, more improvisation, and more authentic ways of being with students.

All the narrative and aesthetic sensibilities that I have discussed are closely related. Intuition and embodied knowing are present in all of them. I found that in the educational literature, little had been written on how to cultivate intuitive, embodied sensibilities in one's teaching. Atkinson and Claxton, in *The Intuitive Practitioner,* maintain that the dominant paradigm in teacher practice and development places more importance on rational, explicit, articulate understanding and reflection and tends to ignore inarticulate, intuitive, implicit ways of knowing and learning.[33] Marilyn Zurmuehlen contends, that "authentic learning is more likely to occur when [art] teachers have the sensibilities of artists."[34]

As I reflected on my years of teaching, I began to understand how I had cultivated narrative and aesthetic sensibilities. First, I saw that vulnerability and gaining knowledge about myself was closely related, if not inseparable. Second, I found that thoughtful self-reflection and reflection with others was essential. Third, I found that participating in close collaboration with other early childhood and art colleagues transformed my teaching, and fourth, I saw that creating time and space for listening and cultivating the ability to see and hear more deeply were essential for enacting a narrative pedagogy.

Vulnerability and Self-Knowledge

One of the most challenging aspects of writing was publicly revealing my mistakes, failures, and weaknesses. Whenever I uncovered a blind spot that kept me from seeing and listening to a child, I felt vulnerable, wondering what others would think of me. However, the areas where I struggled the most, if I dared to understand why, allowed me to grow in understanding the children and myself.

When I first began to think about sharing my views of narrative pedagogy, I thought it would be most useful to share "peak" experiences. I found, though, that when I read the struggles of other early childhood educators,[35] I learned as much from their shortcomings as I did from their successes. I could relate their struggles to my own. As they

---

33 Atkinson and Claxton (2000)
34 Marilyn Zurmuehlen (1986), 36.
35 See for example, Ashton-Warner, 1963; Milne, 2021; Paley, 1986, 1990. Full citations in Bibliography.

interrogated their teaching, they opened space for me to question my teaching as well.

In situations where I am unaware of my shadows, fears, or assumptions, I am not able to balance the mobile—primarily because I am not aware that it is unbalanced. Knowing my limitations, knowing where I have difficulty listening, enables me to be open to possibilities for transformation, for deepening and refining sensibilities of intuition, attentiveness, sympathetic understanding, openness, sensitivity, and thoughtfulness.

Thoughtful Reflection

· Inevitably, as a teacher I make mistakes, but I should not be afraid of this. By remaining reflective and striving to understand the consequences of my actions, I can enter more deeply into the worlds of the children I teach. Thoughtful reflection contributes to a heightened capacity to perceive what is important to children within given pedagogical moments.

Although reflection can take many forms, I found Milne's process of reflective artmaking to be helpful in making visible the unconscious, intuitive thoughts, and feelings. By creating visual images and metaphors, she was able to give aesthetic form to her musings, conflicts, tensions, nonverbalized thoughts, feelings, and perceptions. In *Picturing Learning*, art educator Karen Ernst wrote, "Drawing helped me to look more closely at my students and to question more intently what they were doing."[36] When she created contour line drawings of her students as they worked, she was able to attend to the nuanced qualities of the body gesture, engagement, their struggles, their mood, their ideas, their interactions with others. She accompanied her drawings with her verbal reflections. Attentive drawing allowed a teacher to see qualities in the experience that he or she might not have discerned with just casual observation. For art teachers, such aesthetic forms of reflection allow for visual representations of the intuitive, embodied, and tacit knowledge that shapes our practice. Once visible, these ineffable qualities can be

---

36 Ernst, 1994, 90.

examined for attitudes, beliefs, and responses that might be hindering our capacity to listen and see the life worlds of children.

Poet and educational researcher Anne Sullivan used a poetic form of reflection to sharpen her own pedagogical sensibilities and those of her pre-service education students. Over a period of three weeks, pre-service teachers observed a child that they had difficulty understanding—possibly one who irritated them. After recording the child's behaviors as well as auditory and body language, the pre-service teachers wrote a poem from the child's point of view, capturing fragments of the child's speech. In reporting on this study, Sullivan wrote, "To get under the skin of the other, rather than to simply report observable externals, demanded a deeper sort of attention, an attention that required an imaginative penetration of barriers and that conjoined with empathy."[37] Sullivan's work reminded me of Maxine Greene's words, "imagination…makes empathy possible."[38] Reflection wedded with imagination allows us to see the world through children's eyes and hear through their ears.

For van Manen narrative played an important role in reflection. When teachers encounter a pedagogically charged "moment," there is no time for deciding what to do; they need to act on the spur of the moment. After the fact, however, teachers can ask themselves, "What could I or should I have done?" In the article, *Pedagogy, Virtue, and Narrative Identity in Teaching,* van Manen explained that from the ancient Greeks to the present, the qualities that we speak of as virtues have been portrayed narratively through drama, story, poem, myth, and parable, often by exemplifying individuals who possess or do not possess certain qualities. When we think of teaching as more than a technical craft—when we understand it to be an ethical endeavor—the stories we tell ourselves reveal the virtues we bring to our relationships with children.

In *After Virtue,* Alasdair MacIntyre suggested that through the tradition of storytelling our ethical lives are shaped:

> Asking you what you did and why, saying what I
> did and why, pondering the difference between your

---

37 Sullivan, 2000, 225.
38 Greene, 1995, 3.

account of what I did and my account of what I did,
and vice versa, these are essential constituents of all
but the very simplest and barest of narratives.[39]

When teachers tell narratives about what happened in the classroom
and reflect on them individually and with others, they give an account
of their intentions and actions—why they thought their actions are
"good, responsible, and appropriate or not."[40] Over the years, many of
my friendships have been with early childhood educators. I have met
with them professionally in study groups and socially as friends. As van
Manen suggested, we tended to share our teaching experiences through
anecdotes and stories. Also, as van Manen said, interpreting those
stories is the more difficult aspect of reflection. Like many art teachers,
I did not receive a background in child development in my preservice
preparation. My background consisted of one educational psychology
class that spent one day on theories of cognitive development in
children. Further, as Milne suggested, in elementary schools, teachers
are often isolated from each other. By reflecting with colleagues more
skilled and experienced than myself, I am able to consider alternative
interpretations of the stories I tell myself, and thereby gain a deeper
understanding of my values and beliefs.

Collaboration with Classroom Teachers

Although I learned a great deal from conversations with colleagues
in the study groups that I attended, my collaboration with Alicia offered
a more powerful experience of shared reflection. Over the course of
four years, Alicia and I talked about how she could incorporate the arts
into her teaching. One day I walked into her classroom and as I looked
at the children's work on the walls, I saw how much it represented the
diversity of voices in her classroom. I realized that she had developed
a sense of how to engage children in more authentic art making that
arose out of the children's lived experiences. It dawned on me that as
we worked side by side every week, she had begun to *internalize* new
ways of being with children and of teaching art. It did not come from

---

39 MacIntyre, 203.
40 Van Manen, 161.

reading a book on art education methods or taking a class in "art for the elementary education major." I, too, *internalized* Alicia's way of being with her children. In particular, her gentleness and positivity in handling the children's conflicts.

Similarly, when I collaborated with Charlene, a parent who taught photography and was herself a documentary photographer, I realized that her way of teaching and being with the students flowed out of who she was as an artist. Being open to her approach to teaching photography helped me to internalize new ways of being with my students.

The Importance of Listening

When I was discouraged by discovering beliefs or attitudes that I disliked, I was comforted by Vivian Paley's account of how her pedagogy evolved:

> In my early teaching years I was in the wrong forest. I paid scant attention to the play and did not hear the stories, though once upon a time I must have also imagined such wondrous events."
>
> I was neither a good listener nor an able storyteller when my name became Teacher. What I doubtless knew as a child was buried under piles of disconnected information. I was a stranger in the classroom, grown distant from the thinking of children." [41]

Over the years Paley developed her own way of listening where she observed, listened to, tape recorded, and transcribed the children's conversations and stories in the play corner of her kindergarten classroom. The themes and stories of the children's play could then become the subject matter of the curriculum.

Schultz suggested that the Chinese character "to listen" represented a deeper meaning of listening. The ideogram is comprised of three brushstrokes. The left stroke stands for the ear. The top right stroke symbolizes the head, mind, or brain. The bottom right stroke represents

---

41 Paley, 1986, 5, 15.

the heart. To listen well, one needs to listen with the heart and mind, not just the ear. It is through listening with the heart and mind that a teacher understands the child and his or her point of view. This quality of listening guides a teacher in knowing how to teach, respond, and act.

To cultivate this type of deep listening, I need to reflect on my image of the child. When I am unaware of my image of the child, the pedagogical mobile is likely to become unbalanced. Balancing the narrative and the normative means I need to listen closely to the children's questions, wonderings, theories, and ideas. I need to respect how they make sense of their worlds by offering them multiple possibilities for making their thinking visible. As protagonists in their own learning, children are not mere consumers of facts and ideas. Therefore, I need to prepare learning spaces where they can actively construct meaning, spaces consistent with their sense of time and natural rhythms. Finally, I need to remember that children are filled with curiosity and eager to learn from the moment of life. Therefore, it is my responsibility to keep alive their imagination, sense of wonder, and natural inclination to explore their world. Only by listening to the children and by nurturing my own narrative and aesthetic sensibilities am I able to enter their worlds and learn with them.

Epilogue

As I browsed through books on artist Alexander Calder, I saw the many different images of the mobiles he created. They reminded me of the many versions there can be of a narrative pedagogy—as many as there are styles and personalities of art teachers. When I thought of my art education and early childhood colleagues, many whom I believed enacted a narrative pedagogy in their own way—I saw how much their teacher identity and past and present art experiences influenced their unique approaches to teaching art to young children. One colleague was highly influenced by the Reggio approach; another was committed to standards and DBAE; another was interested in art as visual culture. Regardless of their normative orientation, they all were committed to balancing their normative aims with the interests, ideas, and experiences of the children.

My purpose in portraying and explicating my concept of narrative pedagogy was not to offer a prescription or yet another "method" of teaching art to children. My desire was to come to a deeper understanding of the complex act of balancing the children's narrative with my normative aims in the midst of the daily pressures of schooling.

A narrative pedagogy values, listens to, and welcomes the narrative into the teaching-learning space. When art teachers create space for the children's narrative—and truly enter the children's worlds—and allow the narrative to inform the curriculum, the art classroom becomes a place of wonder, respect, dialogue, passion, stories, imagination, possibility, and joy. My hope is that the lessons that I learned on how to listen more carefully, navigate the tensions more sensitively, and cultivate pedagogical sensibilities more deeply can offer other early childhood art educators greater possibilities for placing the child at the heart of our discipline and for creating art classrooms that dance with "the joy of life."

Bibliography

Arnheim, Rudolf. "The Double-edged Mind: Intuition and the Intellect." In *Learning and Teaching the Ways of Knowing* edited by Elliot W. Eisner, 77-96. Chicago, IL: University of Chicago Press, 1985.

Ashton-Warner, Silvia. *Teacher*. New York: Simon & Schuster, 1963.

Atkinson, Terry, and Guy Claxton, eds. *The Intuitive Practitioner: On the Value of Not Always Knowing What One is Doing.* Philadelphia, PA: Open University Press, 2000.

Ayers, William. *The Good Preschool Teacher*. New York: Teachers College Press, 1989.

Ayers, William. *To Teach: The Journey of a Teacher*. New York: Teachers College Press, 1993.

Barone, Thomas, and Elliot Eisner. "Arts-based educational research." In *Complimentary Methods for Research in Education,* edited by Richard. M. Jaeger, 71-98. Washington, DC: American Education Research Association, 1997.

Barrel, John. *Playgrounds of Our Minds*. New York: Teachers College Press, 1980.

Barrell, Barry. "Classroom Artistry." *The Educational Forum, 55*, no. 4, (1991), 333-342.

Bateson, Mary C. Composing a life. In *Sacred Stories: A Celebration of the Power of Stories to Transform and Heal,* edited by Charles Simpkinson and Anne Simpkinson, 39-52. San Francisco, CA: Harper, 1993.

Bernstein, Basil. "A Critique of the Concept "Compensatory Education." In *Functions of Language in the Classroom*, edited by Courtney B. Cazden, Vera P. John, and Dell Hymes, 135-151. New York: Teachers College Press, 1972.

Bleiker, Charles A. "A Case for Early Art Education: The Development of Self through Art." *Art Education* 51, no. 3 (1999), 48-53.

Block, A. A., & Klein, S. R. "This is Where I Am Right Now: Art Education, Curriculum and Postcards." *Art Education* 49, no. 3 (1996), 20-24.

Bluestein, Jane. *Creating Emotionally Safe Schools*. Deerfield Beach, FL: Health Communications, Inc., 2001.

Bollnow, Otto F. "The Pedagogical Atmosphere: The Perspective of the Child." *Phenomenology + Pedagogy,* 7, (1989), 12-36.

Bredekamp, Sue and Carol E. Copple, eds. *Developmentally Appropriate Practice in Early Childhood Programs Serving Children from Birth through Age 8,* 2nd ed. Washington, DC: National Association for the Education of Young Children, 1997.

Bresler, Liora. "Three Orientations to Arts in the Primary Grades: Implications for Curriculum Reform." *Arts Education Policy Review,* 94, no. 6, (1993), 29-34.

Bresler, Liora. "The Case of the Easter bunny." In *The Visual Arts and Early Childhood Learning,* edited by Christine M. Thompson, 35-39. Reston, VA: National Art Education Association, 1995.

Brown, Robert K. "Max van Manen and Pedagogical Human Science Research." In *Understanding Curriculum as Phenomenological and Deconstructed Text,* edited by William F. Pinar and William M. Reynolds, 44-63. New York: Teachers College Press, 1992.

Brown, Maurice, and Diana Koreznik. *Art Making and Education.* Chicago, IL: University of Chicago Press, 1993.

Bruner, Jerome. *Actual Minds, Possible Worlds.* Cambridge, MA: Harvard University Press, 1986.

Bruner, Jerome. "Life as Narrative." In *The Need for Story: Cultural Diversity in Classroom and Community,* edited by Anne H. Dyson and Celia Genishi, 28-37. Urbana, IL: National Council for Teachers of English, 1994.

Bruner, Jerome. *The Culture of Education.* Cambridge, MA: Harvard University Press, 1996.

Bruner, Jerome. "Some Specifications for a Space to House a Reggio Preschool." In *Children, Spaces, Relations,* edited by Guilio Ceppi and Michele Zini, 137. Reggio Emilia, Italy: Reggio Children, 1998.

Buber, Martin. *Between Man and Man.* New York: Macmillan, 1965.

Buber, Martin. *I and Thou.* New York: Charles Scribner's Sons, 1970.

Burton, Judith M. "The Configuration of Meaning: Learner-centered Art Education Revisite." *Studies in Art Education,* 41, no. 4, (2000), 350-345.

Burton, Judith M. "Lowenfeld: An(other) Look." *Art Education, 54,* no. 6, (2001), 33-42.

Burton, Judith. "Materials and the embodiment of meaning." *Studio Potter, 30*(2), 2002, 67-70.

Cadwell, Louise B. *Bringing Reggio Emilia Home: An Innovative Approach to Early Childhood Education.* New York: Teachers College Press, 1997.

Cadwell, Louise B. *Bringing Learning to Life: A Reggio Approach to Early Childhood Education.* New York: Teachers College Press, 2002.

Carini, Patricia. *The art of seeing and the visibility of the person.* Grand Forks, ND: University of North Dakota Press. 1979.

Carson, Rachel. *A sense of wonder*. Boston: Houghton Mifflin Company. 1955.

Clark, Gilbert A., Michael D. Day, and W. Dwaine Greer.

Discipline-based Art Education: Becoming Students of Art. *Journal of Aesthetic Education* 21, no. 2 (1987), 129-197.

Clarke-Stewart, Alison, and Susan Friedman. *Child Development: Infancy through Adolescence*. New York: Wiley, 1987.

Cobb, Edith. *The Ecology of Imagination in Childhood*. Dallas, TX: Spring Publications, 1977.

Colbert, Cynthia B. "Developmentally Appropriate Practice in Early Art Education." In *The Visual Arts and Early Childhood Learning*, edited by Christine M. Thompson, 35-39. Reston, VA: National Art Education Association, 1995.

Cole, Elizabeth. "A Portrait of an Early Childhood Art Teacher". In *The Visual Arts and Early Childhood Learning*, edited by Christine M. Thompson, 40-43. Reston, VA: National Art Education Association, 1995.

Coles, Robert. "Struggling toward Childhood. An Interview with Robert Coles." *Second Opinion* 18, no. 4 (1993), 58-71.

Connelly, F. Michael, and Jean D. Clandinin. *Teachers as Curriculum Planners: Narratives of Experience*. New York: Teachers College Press, 1988.

Connelly, F. Michael, and Jean D. Clandinin. "Stories of Experience and Narrative inquiry." *Educational Researcher,* 19, no. 5, (1990), 2-14.

Csikszentmihalyi, Mihaly. *Flow: The Psychology of Optimal Experience*. New York: Harper Collins, 1990.

Csikszentmihalyi, Mihaly and Hermanson, Kim. "Intrinsic Motivation in Museums: Why does one want to learn?" In *Public Institutions for Personal Learning: Establishing a Research Agenda*, edited by John H. Falk and Lynn D. Dierking, 67-77. Washington, DC: American Association of Museums, 1995.

Curry, Nancy E., "The Reality of Make-believe." In *Mister Rogers' Neighborhood: Children, Television, and Fred Rogers*, edited by Mark Collins and Margaret M. Kimmel, 51-64. Pittsburgh, PA: University of Pittsburgh Press, 1996.

Curry, Nancy E., and Carl N. Johnson. *Beyond Self-esteem: Developing a Genuine Sense of Human Value*. Washington, DC: National Association for the Education of Young Children, 1990.

Dahlberg, Gunilla, Peter Moss, and Alan Pence. *Beyond Quality in Early Childhood Education and Care: Postmodern Perspectives*. Philadelphia, PA: Falmer Press, 1999.

Darling Hammond, Linda and Jeannie Oakes, *Preparing Teachers for Deeper Learning*. San Francisco: John Wiley & Sons, 2005.

Davis, Jessica. "The 'U' and Wheel of 'C': Development and Devaluation of Graphic Symbolization and the Cognitive Approach at Harvard Project Zero." In *Child*

Development in Art, edited by Anna M. Kindler, 45-58. Reston, VA: National Art Education Association, 1997.

Davis, Jessica, and Howard Gardner. "The Arts and Early Childhood Education: A Cognitive Developmental Portrait of the Young Child as Artist." In *Handbook of Research on the Education of Young Children*, edited by Bernard Spodek, 191-206. New York: Macmillan, 1993.

Deniston-Trochta, Grace. "The Meaning of Storytelling as Pedagogy." *Visual Arts Research, 24*, no. 2, 27-32. 1998.

Delpit, Lisa. *Other people's children: Cultural Conflict in the Classroom*. New York: New Press, 1995.

Deri, Susan. "Transitional Phenomena: Vicissitudes of Symbolization and Creativity."In

Between Reality and Fantasy, edited by Simon Grolnick and Leonard Barkin, 43-60. Northvale, NJ: Jason Aronson, 1978.

Dewey, John. *Democracy and Education*. New York: Macmillan, 1916/1944.

Dewey, John. *How We Think*. New York: D. C. Heath & Co, 1933.

Dewey, John. *Art as Experience*. New York: Putnam, 1934.

Dewey, John. *Education and Experience*. New York: Macmillan, 1938.

Dewey, John. *The School and Society and the Child and the Curriculum*. Chicago, IL: University of Chicago Press, 1902/1990.

Diekelmann, Nancy and John Diekelmann. "Learning Ethics in Nursing and Genetics: Narrative Pedagogy and the Grounding of Values." *Journal of Pediatric Nursing, 15*(4), 226-230, 2000.

Dissanayake, Ellen. "*What is Art For?*" Seattle, WA: University of Washington, 1988.

Donaldson, Margaret, Robert Grieve, and Chris Pratt, eds. *Early Child Development and Education*. New York: Guilford Press, 1983.

Duckworth, E. *The Having of Wonderful Ideas*. New York: Teachers College Press, 1996.

Douglas, Katherine and Diane B. Jaquith, *Engaging Learners through Artmaking*. Teachers College Press, 2009.

Dyson, Anne H. *Multiple Worlds of Child Writers: Friends Learning to Write*. New York: Teachers College Press, 1989.

Dyson, Anne H. "Symbol Makers, Symbol Weavers: How Children Link Play, Pictures, and Print." *Young Children, 45*, no. 2, (1990), 50-57.

Edwards, Carolyn, Lilla Gandini, and George Forman, eds. *The Hundred Languages of Children: The Reggio Emilia Approach—Advanced Reflections,* 2nd ed. Norwood, NJ: Ablex, 1998.

Efland, Arthur D. "The School Art Style: A Functional Analysis." *Studies in Art Education, 17*(2), (1976), 37-44.

Efland, Arthur D. *A History of Art Education.* New York: Teachers College Press, 1990.

Efland, Arthur D. "The Entwined Nature of the Aesthetic: A Discourse on Visual Culture." *Studies in Art Education,* 45, no. 3, (2004), 234-251.

Egan, Kieran. *Teaching as Storytelling: An Alternative Approach to Teaching and Curriculum in the Elementary School.* Chicago, IL: University of Chicago Press, 1989.

Egan, Kieran, and Dan Nadaner. *Imagination and Education.* New York: Teachers College Press, 1988.

Eisner, Elliot W. *The Educational Imagination.* New York: Macmillan, 1979.

Eisner, Elliot W. "The Primacy of Experience and the Politics of Method." *Educational Researcher,,* 17, no. 5, (1988), 15-20

Eisner, Elliot W. *The Enlightened Eye: Qualitative Inquiry and the Enhancement of Educational Practice.* New York: Macmillan, 1991.

Eisner, Elliot W. "The Emergence of New Paradigms for Educational Research." *Art Education,* 46, no. 6, (1993), 50-55

Eisner, Elliot W. "What Artistically Crafted Research Can Help Us Understand about Schools." *Educational Theory,* 45, no. 1, (1995), 1-6.

Eisner, Elliot W. Cognition and Representation. *Phi Delta Kappan,* 78(5), (1997), 349-353.

Eisner, Elliot W. *The Kind of Schools We Need.* Portsmouth, NH: Heinemann, 1998.

Eisner, Elliot W. *The Arts, Human Development, and Education: Recent Reflections.* Transcription of keynote address presented at the Arts in Early Education: A Policy Conference. Shady Lane Preschool, Pittsburgh, PA, 2000.

Eisner, Elliot W." Should we create new aims for art education?" *Art Education,* 54(5), (2000), 6-10.

Eisner, Elliot W. "What Can Education Learn from the Arts about the Practice of Education?" *Journal of Curriculum and Supervision* 18, no. 1, (2002), 4-16.

Ernst, Karen. *Picturing Learning: Artists and Writers in the Classroom.* Portsmouth, NH: Heinemann, 1994.

Fahey, Patrick. "Magic eyes: Transforming Teaching through First Grade Sketchbooks." *Visual Arts Research,* 22, no. 1, (1996), 34-43.

Flickenger, Aprile. "Therapeutic listening." *Phenomenology + Pedagogy* 10, (1992), 186-193.

Forman, George. "The Constructivist Perspective to Early Education." In *Approaches to Early Childhood Education* edited by Jaipaul Roopnarine and James Johnson, 102-121. Columbus, OH: Merrill, 1992.

Forman, George. "The Project Approach in Reggio Emilia." In *Constructivism: Theory, Perspectives and Practice*, edited by Catherine Fosnot, 172-181. New York: Teachers College Press, 1996.

Forman, George, and Fyfe, Brenda. "Negotiated Learning through Design, Documentation, and Discourse." In *The hundred languages of children: The Reggio Emilia approach—advanced reflections,* 2nd ed., edited by Carolyn Edwards, Lella Gandini, and George Forman, 239-260. Norwood, NJ: Ablex, 1998.

Franklin, Margery B. "Meanings of Play in the Developmental-interaction Tradition." In *Revisiting a Progressive Pedagogy: The Developmental-interaction Approach,* edited by Nancy Nager and Edna K. Shapiro, 47-71. Albany, NY: State University of New York Press, 2000.

Frellare, Paulo. *Pedagogy of the Oppressed.* New York: Herder and Herder, 1970.

Froebel, Friedrich. *The Education of Man,* translated by William N. Hailmann. Clifton,NJ: Augustus M. Kelly, 1974.

Gallas, Karen. *Imagination and Literacy.* New York: Teachers College Press, 2003.

Gandini, Lella. "Fundamentals of the Reggio Emilia Approach to Early Childhood Education". *Young Children* 49, no. 1 (1993), 4-8.

Gandini, Lella. "Educational and Caring Spaces." In *The Hundred Languages of Children: The Reggio Emilia Approach—Advanced Reflections, 2nd ed,* edited by Carolyn Edwards, Lella Gandini, and George Forman, 161-178. Norwood, NJ: Ablex, 1998.

Gardner, Howard. *Frames of Mind: The Theory of Multiple Intelligences.* New York: Basic Books, 1983.

Garman, Noreen. B. "The Drama of the Classroom: Dramaturgy as Curriculum Inquiry. In *Reflections from the Heart of Educational Inquiry: Understanding Curriculum and Teaching through the Arts,* edited by George Willis, and William H. Schubert, 277-283. Albany, New York: State University of New York Press, 1991.

Garman, Noreen B. *Studying One's Practice through Qualitative Dissertation Research: Solipsism or Scholarship?* Paper presented at the American Educational Research Association Annual Meeting, Seattle, Washington, April 2001.

Garman, Noreen. B., and Maria Piantanida, eds, *The Authority to Imagine: The Struggle toward Method in Dissertation Writing.* Oakmont: Learning Moments Press, 2018.

Gaudelius, Yvonne and Peg Speirs, eds. *Contemporary Issues in Art Education.* Upper Saddle River, NJ: Prentice-Hall, 2002.

Genishi, Celia, ed. *Ways of Assessing Children and Curriculum.* New York: Teachers College Press, 1992.

Gerity, Lani A. *Creativity and the Dissociative Patient: Puppets, Narrative, and Art in the Treatment of Survivors of Childhood Trauma.* London: Jessica Kingsley Publishers, 1992.

Gerity, Lani A. "Josie, Winnicott, and the hungry ghosts." *Art Therapy: Journal of the Art Therapy Association* 18, no. 1 (2001), 44-49.

Giles, Amy R. *"Making Special": Child-centered, Meaningful, and Artistically Authentic Early Childhood Art Education.* Unpublished doctoral dissertation, University of Illinois at Urbana-Champaign, 2000.

Giroux, Henry A. and Roger I. Simon, eds. *Popular Culture, Schooling, and Everyday Life.* Massachusetts: Bergin & Garvey Publishers, Inc., 1989.

Goldberg, Merryl R., and Ann Phillips." Introduction." In *Arts in Education.*, edited by Merryl R. Goldberg and Ann Phillips, Cambridge, MA: Harvard Educational Review, 1992.

Goodman, Nelson. *Ways of Worldmaking.* Indianapolis, IN: Hackett Publishing Co., 1978.

Greene, Maxine. *Landscapes of Learning.* New York: Teachers College Press, 1978.

Greene, Maxine. "Blue Guitars and the Search for Curriculum." In *Reflections from the Heart of Educational Inquiry: Understanding Curriculum and Teaching through the Arts,* edited by George Willis and William H. Schubert, 102-122. Albany, New York: State University of New York Press, 1991.

Greene, Maxine. *Releasing the Imagination: Essays on Education, the Arts, and Social Change.* San Francisco, CA: Jossey-Bass, 1995.

Greene, Maxine. "Metaphors and Multiples: Representation, the Arts, and History." *Phi Delta Kappan* 78, no. 5 (1997), 387-394.

Greenspan, Stanley I. *The Growth of the Mind.* New York: Addison-Wesley, 1997.

Greer, W. Dwaine. "A Structure of Discipline Concepts for DBAE." *Studies in Art Education 28*, no. 4 (1987), 227-233.

Greishaber, Susan J., and Carmel M. Diezmann. "The Challenge of Teaching and Learning Science with Young Children." In *Promoting Meaningful Learning,* edited by Nicola J. Yelland, 87-94. Washington, DC: National Association for the Education of Young Children, 2000.

Guidici, Claudia, Mara Krechevsky, and Carlina Rinaldi, eds. *Making learning visible: Children as individual and group learners.* Reggio Emilia, Italy: Reggio Children, 2001.

Gwathmey, Edith and Ann-Marie Mott. "Visualizing Experience." In *Revisiting a Progressive Pedagogy: The Developmental-interaction Approach* edited by Nancy Nager and Edith K. Shapiro, 139-160. Albany, NY: State University of New York Press, 2000.

Hamblen, Karen A. "The Emergence of Neo-DBAE." In *Art Education: Content and Practice in a Postmodern Era,* edited by James W. Hutchens and Marianne S. Suggs, 40-46. Reston, VA: National Art Education Association, 1997.

Hankins, Karen H. *Teaching through the Storm: A Journey of Hope.* New York: Teachers College Press, 2003.

Hargreaves, Andy. *Changing Teachers, Changing Times.* New York: Teachers College Press, 1994.

Heshusius, Lous. "Freeing Ourselves from Objectivity: Managing Subjectivity or Turning toward a Participatory Mode of Consciousness." *Educational Researcher* 23, no. 3 (1994): 15-22.

Heshusius, Lous and Keith Ballard, eds. *From Positivism to Interpretivism and Beyond.* New York: Teachers College Press, 1996.

Hopkins, Richard L. *Narrative Schooling: Experiential Learning and the Transformation of American Education.* New York: Teachers College Press, 1994.

Hubbard Ruth Shagaury and Brenda Miller Power. *Living the Questions.* York, Maine: Stenhouse Publishers, 1999.

Isaacs, William. *Dialogue and the Art of Thinking Together.* New York: Doubleday, 1999.

Jagla, Virginia M. *Teachers' Everyday Use of Imagination and Intuition.* New York: State University of New York Press, 1994.

Janson, Horst W. *History of Art,* 3rd ed. New York: Harry N. Abrams, 1986.

Jones, Elizabeth and Gretchen Reynolds. *The Play's the Thing: Teachers' Roles in Children's Play.* New York: Teachers College Press, 1992.

Katch, Jane. *Under Deadman's Skin: Discovering the Meaning of Children's Violent Play.* Boston, MA: Beacon Press, 2001.

Keller, Evelyn Fox. *A Feeling for the Organism: The Life and Work of Barbara McClintock.* New York: W. H. Freeman & Company, 1983.

Kellman, Julia. The Case for Developmentally Appropriate Lessons: The Child and Art. *Visual Arts Research* 20, no. 2, 1994, 62-68.

Kellman, Julia. "Harvey Shows the Way: Narrative in Children's Art." *Art Education,* 48, no. 2 (1995), 18-22.

Kerlavage, Marianne. *Artworks and Young Children: An Historical Analysis of the Paradigm Governing the Use of Art Appreciation in Early Childhood.* Unpublished Doctoral Dissertation, University of Wisconsin/Milwaukee, 1992.

Kerlavage, Marianne. "A Bunch of Naked Ladies and a Tiger: Children's Responses to Adult Works of Art." In *The Visual Arts and Early Childhood Learning*, edited by Christine M. Thompson, 56-62. Reston, VA: National Art Education Association, 1995.

Kilbourn, B. "Reflecting on Vignettes of Teaching." In *Reflection in Teacher Education,* edited by Peter P. Grimmett and Gaalen L. Erickson, 91-111. New York: Teachers College Press, 1988.

Kincheloe, Joe L., Patrick Slattery, and Shirley R. Steinberg, *Contextualizing Teaching.* New York: Addison Wesley Longman, 2000.

Kindler, Anna M. "Significance of Adult Input in Early Childhood Artistic Development." In *The Visual Arts and Early Childhood Learning.* edited by Christine M. Thompson, 10-14. Reston, VA: National Art Education Association, 1995.

Kohl, Herbert. Forward. In *The Grammar of Fantasy: The Art of Inventing* Stories, edited by Gianni Rodari, ix-xi. New York: Teachers & Writers Collaborative, 1996.

Krechevsky, Mara, and Janet Stork. "Challenging Educational Assumptions: Lessons from an Italian-American Collaboration." *Cambridge Journal of Education,* 30, no.1 (2000): 57-74.

Langer, Susanne. *Philosophy in a New Key.* Cambridge, MA: Harvard University Press, 1942.

Leeds, Jo Alice. "Teaching and the Reasons for Making Art." *Art Education* 39, no. 4 (1986): 17-21.

Lipman, Jean. *Calder's Universe.* Philadelphia, PA: Running Press Book Publishers, 1976.

Logsdon, Marjorie B. *A Pedagogy of Authority.* Oakmont: Learning Moments Press, 2017.

Lowenfeld, Viktor. *Creative and Mental Growth.* New York: Macmillan, 1957.

Lyons, Nona, and Vicki K. LaBoskey, eds. *Narrative Inquiry in Practice.* New York: Teachers College Press, 2002.

MacIntyre, Alasdair. *After Virtue.* Notre Dame, IN: University of Notre Dame Press, 1981.

Malaguzzi, Loris. "For an Education Based on Relationships." *Young Children* 49, no. 1 (1993), 33-36.

Malaguzzi, Loris. "Your Image of the Child: Where Teaching Begins." *Child Care Information Exchange, 96* (1994): 52-56.

Malaguzzi, Loris. "No Way the Hundred Is There." In *The Hundred Languages of Children: The Reggio Emilia Approach—Advanced Reflections,* 2nd ed, edited by Carolyn Edwards, Lella Gandini, and George Forman, 2-3. Norwood, NJ: Ablex, 1998.

Matthews, Gareth B. *The Philosophy of Childhood.* Cambridge, MA: Harvard University Press, 1984.

May, Wanda T. "The Arts and Curriculum as Lingering." In *Reflections from the Heart of Educational Inquiry: Understanding Curriculum and Teaching through the Arts,* edited by George Willis and William H. Schubert, 140-152. Albany, New York: State University of New York Press, 1991.

May, Wanda T. "Teachers as Curriculum Developers." In *Context, Content, and Community in Art Education: Beyond Postmodernism,* edited by In Ron W. Neperud, 53-86. New York: Teachers College Press, 1995.

McEwan, Helena, and Kieran Egan, eds, *Narrative in Teaching, Learning, and Research.* New York: Teachers College Press, 1995.

McMahon, Patricia L. *A Narrative Study of Levels of Reflection in a College Composition Class: Teacher Journal, Student Portfolios, Teacher-student Discourse.* Unpublished doctoral dissertation, University of Pittsburgh,1993.

Milne, Wendy M. *Professional Learning through Reflective Artmaking: A Pedagogical Portfolio.* Oakmont: Learning Moments Press, 2021.

Mims, Sandra K., and E. Louis Lankford. "The New Art Education and What We've Learned from Superwoman." *Art Education 47*(3), 1994, 57-61.

Mims, Sandra K., and E. Louis Lankford. "Time, Money, and the New Art Education: A Nationwide Investigation." *Studies in Art Education, 36*(2), 1995, 84-95.

Mitchell, Lucie Sprague. *Young Geographers.* New York: Basic Books, 1934.

Montessori, Jr. Mario. *Education for Human Development: Understanding Montessori.* New York: Schocken Books, 1976.

National Art Education Association. *Standards for Art Teacher Preparation.* Reston, VA: National Art Education Association, 1999.

Nehls, N. (1995). "Narrative Pedagogy: Rethinking Nursing Education." *Journal of Nursing Education, 34*(5), 204-210.

Neperud, Ron W. "Transitions in Art Education: A Search for Meaning." In *Context, Content, and Community in Art Education: Beyond Postmodernism*, edited by Ron W. Neperud, 1-22. New York: Teachers College Press, 1995.

Noddings, Nel., and Paul J. Shore. *Awakening the Inner Eye: Intuition in Education.* New York: Teachers College Press, 1984.

Oldfather, Penny and Jane West. *Learning through Children's Eyes: Social Constructivism and the Desire to Learn.* Washington, DC: American Psychological Association, 1999.

Paley, Vivian G." On Listening to What Children Say." *Harvard Educational Review* 56, no. 2, (1986), 122-131.

Paley, Vivian G. *The Boy Who Would Be a Helicopter: The Uses of Storytelling in the Classroom.* Cambridge, MA: Harvard University Press, 1990.

Palmer, Parker J. *The Courage to Teach.* San Francisco, CA: Jossey-Bass, 1998.

Papert, Seymour. *Mindstorms.* New York: Basic Books, 1982.

Perkins, David N. "Creativity by Design." *Educational Leadership* 42, no. 1 (1984):18-25.

Percy, Walker. *The Moviegoer.* New York: The Noonday Press, 1961.

Piantanida, Maria, and Noreen B. Garman. *The Qualitative Dissertation: A Guide for Students and Faculty, 2nd ed.* Thousand Oaks, CA: Corwin Press, 2009.

Polanyi, Michael. *Personal Knowledge.* Chicago, IL: University of Chicago Press, 1958.

Polanyi, Michael. *The Tacit Dimension.* London: Routledge and Kegan Paul, 1967.

Rankin, Baji M. *Collaboration as the Basis of Early Childhood Curriculum Development: A Case Study from Reggio Emilia, Italy.* Unpublished doctoral dissertation, Boston University, 1995.

Richards, Lynn A. *Pictures in our Minds: A Narrative Study of the Incorporation of Creative Dramatics Pedagogy in Elementary Classroom Content Areas.* Unpublished doctoral dissertation, University of Pittsburgh., 1996.

Richardson, Laurel. *Writing strategies: Reaching Diverse Audiences.* (Qualitative Research Methods Series 21). Newbury Park, CA: Sage Publications, 1990.

Rilke, Rainer Maria. *Letters to a Young Poet,* translated by Mary D. Herter Norton. New York: Norton, 1993.

Rinaldi, Carlina. "The Emergent Curriculum and Social Constructivism." In *The Hundred Languages of Children: The Reggio Emilia Approach to Early Childhood Education, edited* by Carolyn Edwards, Lella Gandini, and George Forman, 101-11, Norwood, NJ: Ablex, 1993.

Rinaldi, Carlina. "Documentation and Assessment: What is the relationship?" In *Making Learning Visible: Children as Individual and Group Learners,* edited by Claudia M. Guidici, Mara Krechevsky and Carlina Rinaldi, 78-89. Reggio Emilia, Italy: Reggio Children, 2001.

Rinaldi, Carlina. "Reggio Emilia: The Image of the Child and the Child's Environment as a Fundamental Principle." In *Bambini: The Italian Approach to Infant/Toddler Care,* edited by Lella Gandini and Carolyn P. Edwards, 49-54. New York: Teachers College Press, 2001b.

Rodari, Gianni. *The Grammar of Fantasy: An Introduction to the Art of Inventing Stories.* New York: Teachers and Writers Collaborative, 1996.

Rubin, Louis J. *Artistry in Teaching.* New York: Random House, 1985.

Schoenfielder, Lisa. *Searching for the Shape of Content in a Studio Based Approach to Art Education.* Unpublished doctoral dissertation, University of Iowa, 1996.

Schultz, Karen. *Listening: A Framework for Teaching across Differences.* New York: Teachers College Press, 2003.

Schubert, William H. *Curriculum: Perspective, Paradigm, and Possibility.* New York: Macmillan, 1986.

Schwartz, Barry and Kenneth Sharpe. *Practical Wisdom: The Right Way to Do the Right Thing.* New York: Riverhead Books, 2010.

Singer, Dorothy G., and Tracey A. Revenson. *A Piaget Primer: How a Child Thinks.* New York: Penguin Books, 1978.

Singer, Dorothy, and Jerome T. Singer. *The House of Make-believe: Children's Play and the Developing Imagination.* Cambridge, MA: Harvard University Press, 1990.

Smith, Nancy R. *Experience and Art: Teaching Children to Paint.* New York: Teachers College Press, 1983.

Smith-Shank, Deborah L. Mickey Mouse or Mapplethorpe: "Metaphors for Understanding Art Anxiety." In *Preservice Art Education: Issues and Practice,* edited by Lynn Galbraith, 31-44. Reston, VA: National Art Education Association, 1995.

Stankiewicz, Mary A. *Roots of Art Education Practice*. Worcester, MA: Davis Publications, 2001.

Steinberg, Shirley R., and Joe L. Kincheloe. *Kinderculture: The Corporate Construction of Childhood*. Boulder, CO: Westview Press, 1997.

Stewart, John. "Forward". In *The Reach of Dialogue: Confirmation, Voices, and Community*, edited by Rob Anderson, Rob Cissna, and Kenneth N. Arnett, viii-xx. Cresskill, New Jersey: Hampton Press, Inc., 1994.

Stinson, Susan W. "Dance as Curriculum, Curriculum as Dance." In *Reflections from the Heart of Educational Inquiry: Understanding Curriculum and Teaching through the Arts*, edited by George Willis and William H. Schubert, 190-196. Albany, New York: State University of New York Press, 1991.

Stinson, Susan W. "What We Teach Is Who We Are." *Visual Arts Research, 25*(2), 2000, 69-78.

Sullivan, Anne. "Notes from A Marine Biologist's Daughter: On the Art and Science of Attention." *Harvard Educational Review* 70, no. 2, (2000), 211-227.

Szekely, George. *From Play to Art*. Portsmouth, NH: Heinemann, 1991.

Tansey Richard G., and Fred S. Kleiner, eds. *Gardner's Art through the Ages, 2nd ed.* New York: Harcourt, Brace & Company, 1996.

Tarr, Patricia. "Reflections on the Image of the Child: Reproducer of Culture or Creator of Culture." *Art Education 56, no.* 4, (2003): 6-11.

Tarr, Patricia. Untitled. Early childhood art education column. *NAEA News, 45*(5), (2003, October), 15.

Taunton, Martha. "Aesthetic Responses of Young Children to the Visual Arts: A Review of Literature." *Journal of Aesthetic Education, 16*(3), 1982, 93-109.

Thompson, Christine M. "The Visual Arts and Early Childhood Learning: Changing Contexts and Concepts." In *The Visual Arts and Early Childhood Learning,* edited by Christine M. Thompson, 1-5. Reston, VA: National Art Education Association, 1995a.

Thompson, Christine M. "Transforming the Curriculum in the Visual Arts." In *Reaching Potentials: Transforming Early Childhood Curriculum and Assessment, vol. 2,* edited by Sue Bredekamp and Theresa Rosegrant, 81-98. Washington, DC: National Association for the Education of Young Children, 1995.

Thompson, Christine M. "What Should I Draw Today?": Sketchbooks in early childhood. *Art Education, 48*(5), 1995, 1-11.

Thompson, Christine. M. "Teaching Art in Elementary Schools: Shared Responsibilities and Distinctive Roles." *Arts Education Policy Review, 99(*2), 1997 ,15-21.

Thompson, Christine M. "Drawing Together: Peer Influence in Preschool-Kindergarten Art Classes," *Visual Arts Research,* 25, no. 2 (2000), 61-68.

Thompson, Christine M. "Kinderculture in the Art Classroom: Early Childhood Art and the Mediation of Culture." *Studies in Art Education* 44, no. 2 (2003), 135-146.

Thunder-McGuire, Steve. *Narrative Accounts of Children's Artists' Bookmaking.* Unpublished Doctoral dissertation. The University of Iowa, 1990.

Tobin, Joseph, Ed. *Making a Place for Pleasure in Early Childhood Education.* New Haven: Yale University Press, 1997.

Tompkins, Jane. "Pedagogy of the Distressed." *College English 52, no.* 6 (1991): 653-660.

Townley, Roderick. Fred's Shoes: "The Meaning of Transitions in *Mister Rogers' Neighborhood.*" In *Mister Rogers' Neighborhood: Children, Television, and Fred Rogers,* edited by Mark Collins and Margaret M. Kimmel, 67-76. Pittsburgh, PA: University of Pittsburgh Press, 1996.

van Manen, Max. *The Tone of Teaching.* Portsmouth, NH: Heinemann, 1986.

van Manen, Max. *The Tact of Teaching: The Meaning of Pedagogical Thoughtfulness.* Albany, NY: State University of New York Press, 1991.

van Manen, Max. *Pedagogy, Virtue and Narrative Identity in Teaching.* Albany, NY: State University of New York Press, 1994.

van Manen, Max. *In Search of the Pedagogical Dimension of Curriculum.* (Cassette Recording No. 210410-17 A-B). Washington, DC: American Education Research Association, 2001.

Vecchi, Vea. *The Theatre Curtain.* Paper presented at the Children, Spaces, and Relations Conference, Cyert Center for Early Childhood Education, Pittsburgh, PA, 2000.

Walling, Donovan R. "Rethinking Visual Arts Education." *Phi Delta Kappan, 82*(8), (2001), 626-630.

Welty, Eudora. *One Writer's Beginnings.* Cambridge, MA: Harvard University Press, 1983.

Wilson, Brent. "The Superheroes of J. C. Holz: Plus, an Outline of a Theory of Child Art." *Art Education* 27, no. 8, (1974), 2-9.

Wilson, Brent. *Manga, the Japanese Curriculum.* Paper presented at the National Art Education Association (NAEA) National Convention, Miami Beach, Florida, 2000.

Winnicott, Donald W. *Playing and Reality.* London: Tavistock Publications, 1971.

Yinger, Robert. "The Intelligence of Practice." In *Images of Reflection in Teacher Education,* edited by Hersh Waxman, Jerome Freiberg, Joseph C. Vaughan, and Marsha Weil. Reston, VA: The Association of Teacher Education, 1988.

Zimmerman, Enid, and Laura Zimmerman. "Art Education and Early Childhood Education: The Young Child as Creator and Meaning Maker within a Community Context." *Young Children,* 55, no. 6, (2000), 87-92.

Zurmuehlen, Marilyn. J. "Reflecting on the Ordinary: Interpretation as Transformation of Experiences." *Art Education, 39*(6), (1986): 33-36.

Zurmuehlen, Marilyn J. *Studio Art: Praxis, Symbol, Presence*. Reston, VA: National
    Art Education Association, 1990.

Acknowledgements

First and foremost, I would like to thank Maria Piantanida, my editor and publisher, for her tireless work in bringing this book to fruition. She has an amazing ability to see a study and transform the ideas into book form that is accessible to lay persons and academics alike. Maria, if it wasn't for you, this book would not exist. I'd also like to thank Mike Murray for his technical expertise in laying out the format of the book and also for finalizing the book cover. I wish I had your skills!

I'd like to thank Noreen Garman and the Writing Study Group that met around Noreen's dining room table to share a meal and offer invaluable insights about my dissertation study. Your support and thoughtful reflections helped me through the process in both dissertation writing and post-doc writing. I especially extend my thanks to Noreen and Maria, and to study group members Pat McMahon, Robin Grubs, Wendy Milne, Lynn Richards, Marilyn Llewellyn, Micheline Stabile, Barb Stevens, Cindy Tananis, Kathy Ceroni, Kathy Gaberson, Helen Hazi, Mary Sciulli, and Leonora Kevuva.

Thank you to my dear friend, Penny Fahlman, for your willingness to meet for coffee and deliberate about my initial study, and for your commitment to reading drafts of my study, giving thoughtful, detailed comments.

To Lucia Webb, thank you for your flexibility and your love of the Reggio Approach I appreciated our collaborations and your letting me work so closely with your students.

To all the kindergarten and primary-age children at the Falk Laboratory School, I wish you knew how much you taught me over the years, not only for this study. You taught me how to listen to what was important to you and how to let your interests inform the curriculum. You allowed me to document your thinking which provided me with so much insight into your interests, personalities, emotional concerns, and unique ideas. I love your ideas, your play, your imaginations—please continue to keep these alive.

To all my colleagues at Falk. I always felt that I could walk into each of your classrooms and learn so much from you. And I did!! A special feeling of gratitude toward Laurie, Marian, Lucia, Nabilah, Amy, Kevin, Krista, Chelsea, Diana, Carolyn, Megan, Kevin G., Becka, and Jill, for inviting me into your primary classrooms and entrusting me with your young students. I'd also like to thank the three directors that I worked under at Falk—Bill MacDonald, for making it possible for me to go on a study tour of the Reggio Emilia schools; Wendell McConnaha, for your support of the art program and me over the years; and Jeff Suzik, for your deep respect of Progressive teaching/learning and making it happen at Falk. You three have been inspirations to me.

A special thanks to the continued support of my sisters—Linda, Paula, Karen, and Becky. Ever since I was in preschool, I was inspired by your thirst for knowledge, your humor, your hunger for reading books. I used to play school at home for hours after you left for school. Is it any wonder that I pursued teaching as a career? I can't thank you enough for your concerns and care towards me during my recent illness and your sincere anticipation for reading my book.

And last but definitely not least, a heart of gratitude and love toward my husband, Jay Armstrong. When I am weak, you are very strong. When I am frustrated, you use humor to make me smile. Thank you for your encouragement, support, positivity, technical expertise, and patience during the writing of this book, and when it is all done, we will spend all of our time with Evie and Immy, our two grandbabies.

About the Author

Pamela Grace Krakowski, Ed.D is a clinical assistant professor at the University of Pittsburgh, School of Education. In 2021, she retired from Falk School, University's laboratory school, where she taught K-5 art. Previously she taught art to students with blindness, ages 2-21, at the Western Pennsylvania School for Blind Children for eleven years. From 1978-2010, she was a part-time museum educator in the Children's Studio at the Carnegie Museum of Art. She has been an active member of the Reggio-Pittsburgh Collaborative and was a past president of the Early Childhood Art Educators (ECAE), an issues group within the National Art Education Association. In 2017 she was awarded the Outstanding Pre-School-12 Educator Award by the University of Pittsburgh's School of Education Alumni Association, and in 2019 she was honored by the National Art Education Association as Outstanding Elementary Art Educator in Pennsylvania.

LEARNING MOMENTS PRESS

L earning Moments Press is the publishing arm of the Scholar-Practitioner Nexus, an online community of individuals committed to the quality of education. Learning Moments Press features three series of books.

The Wisdom of Practice Series showcases the work of individuals who illuminate the complexities of practice as they strive to fulfill the purpose of their profession.

The Wisdom of Life Series offers insightful reflections on significant life events that challenge the meaning of one's life, one's sense of self, and one's place in the world.

The Social Context Series showcases the work of individuals who illuminate the macro socio-economic-political contexts within which education policy and practice are enacted.

Cooligraphy artist Daniel Nie created the logo for Learning Moments Press by combining two symbol systems. Following the principles of ancient Asian symbols, Daniel framed the logo with the initials of Learning Moments Press. Within this frame, he has replicated the Adinkra symbol for *Sankofa* as interpreted by graphic artists at the Documents and Design Company. As explained by Wikipedia, Adinkra is a writing system of the Akan culture of West Africa. *Sankofa* symbolizes taking from the past what is good and bringing it into the present in order to make positive progress through the benevolent use of knowledge. Inherent in this philosophy is the belief that the past illuminates the present and that the search for knowledge is a life-long process.

www.ingramcontent.com/pod-product-compliance
Lightning Source LLC
Chambersburg PA
CBHW070703130626

46553CB00005B/1815